"*Dream Dreams* by Steve and Dianne Bydeley re-opens the door to hearing God through your dreams. Many will learn to receive God's counsel at night through their dreams as a result of this book, making it a priceless gift to the body of Christ. After hundreds of years of not taking dreams seriously, pioneers such as Steve and Dianne are laying a groundwork for the restoration of a biblical view and experience of dreams. More light will continue to be added as we go along, but this book is a shining beacon to move people on in the right direction. Thank you, Steve and Dianne, for your gift to the Church. May God enlarge your ministry as you teach this widely."

Dr. Mark Virkler
Communion With God Ministries
President of Christian Leadership University

"There is a hunger for supernatural revelation. The Spirit of God is releasing key revelation that will uncover His redemptive plan in the world. The Bible is coming alive as the voice of God teaches us to understand times and seasons. We must not be afraid of the supernatural. Dreams will become very significant in God's plan to unlock harvest throughout the world. *Dream Dreams* is such an important book for the hour. Joel 2:28–29 says: "*And it shall come to pass afterward that I will pour out my Spirit on all flesh; and your sons and your daughters shall prophesy, your old men shall dream dreams, your young men shall see visions. And also upon the servants and upon the handmaids in those days will I pour out my spirit.*" This is God's restorative plan for His people in days ahead. This book helps us to enter into this plan."

Dr. Chuck D. Pierce
Vice-president, Global Harvest Ministries
President, Glory of Zion International, Inc.

Dream Dreams

Open the door to the biblical interpretation of dreams and visions

Essence
PUBLISHING

Belleville, Ontario, Canada

Dream Dreams

*Open the door to the biblical interpretation
of dreams and visions*

Copyright © 2002, Steve and Dianne Bydeley

All Scripture quotations, unless otherwise specified, are taken from the
Updated New American Standard Bible, copyright © The Lockman Foundation 1960, 1962, 1963, 1968, 1971, 1972, 1973, 1975, 1977, 1995. All
rights reserved.

Scriptures marked NIV are from *The Holy Bible, New International Version.* Copyright © 1973, 1978, 1984 International Bible Society. Used by
permission of Zondervan Publishing House. All rights reserved.

Scripture quotations marked NLT are taken from *The Holy Bible,* New
Living Translation. Copyright © 1996. Used by permission of Tyndale
House Publishers, Inc., Wheaton, IL 60187. All rights reserved.

ISBN: 1-55306-381-3

Essence Publishing is a Christian Book Publisher dedicated to
furthering the work of Christ through the written word.
For more information, contact:
44 Moira Street West, Belleville, Ontario, Canada K8P 1S3.
Phone: 1-800-238-6376. Fax: (613) 962-3055.
E-mail: info@essencegroup.com
Internet: www.essencegroup.com

Printed in Canada
by

Essence
PUBLISHING

This book is dedicated to those
in the body of Christ who are searching
for a closer relationship with God.

Our thanks and appreciation go to the many
friends who helped work through the manuscript,
offered direction, and gave encouragement:
Rev. Art Zeilstra, Ontario, Canada;
Dr. and Mrs. Stan Gentz, BC, Canada;
Graham Gilmore, Sydney, Australia;
Dr. Derek Morphew, Cape Town, South Africa;
Dr. and Mrs. Gordon Fee, BC, Canada;
Dr. David Clements, BC, Canada;
and others.

Most of all we are thankful, with our whole
beings, to the giver of dreams—God our savior, Jesus.

Contents

Part II — Interpreting...

Foreword

ream Dreams is a gem of a book. It is one of those books that is seemingly specific in focus, but ends up being a real tool for life. Because God is love, he loves to commune and communicate with his people. Although dreams are one of the primary ways in which God communicates with his people, there has been a definite lack of solid, practical, and biblically-based books on the topic. Because so much of the revelation God desires to give his sons and daughters involves bringing us into a more abundant life, this book, I would say, should be a studied book in every Christian's library.

I first met Dianne about ten years ago. She has always demonstrated a true heart for God, his ways, and serving him. After not seeing her for some six years, I recently met her and her husband, Steve, while ministering in Sydney,

Australia. Steve, too, exudes both a passion for God and a love for people. In the few years since I had last spoken with Dianne, she and Steve had developed great insight and wisdom in the area of dreams and recognizing how God speaks through dreams. I would wholeheartedly encourage all who hope to grow in their working knowledge of the prophetic to read and study *Dream Dreams*. Even more, however, I would encourage all who hope to grow in intimacy with God to get ahold of it. For many it will be a source of wisdom and encouragement, but for some, I suspect, it will be a life-changing tool as they learn to really know, in a sound and biblical way, what the Holy Spirit is trying to release into their lives.

Marc A. Dupont
Mantle of Praise Ministries, Inc.
Ft. Wayne, Indiana
March 9, 2002

Preface

$\mathcal{M}$y (Steve's) interest in dreams jumped dramatically some years ago when I awoke, eyes wide open, from a dream. The symbolism in that dream shocked me. I did not know its meaning, but I knew there was a message in it for me, and so I leapt out of bed to write it down and slept little after that.

In the months before that dream, I had been under much emotional stress. The symbolism obviously related to that ordeal. Wanting to understand the message of the dream, I called Rev. Art Zeilstra, our friend and founder of Cornerstone Christian Counseling Center where we are associates. At his suggestion, we met to try a listening prayer approach, hoping to receive insight to the dream. This approach proved to be very effective in understanding the dream. Although I cannot go into the details, the dream proved to be important to my well-being. It helped me handle the stress I was experiencing. Much of the burden was lifted, enabling me to get on with life.

We believe God desires relationship with his children, both individually and corporately. It is through the death and resurrection of his son, Jesus, and the person of the Holy Spirit that we can approach him as our Father. In that role—Father—he is interested in the details and events of our lives. This intimate involvement in the lives of his children is called *relationship*. Culturally, socially, and spiritually, have we wasted a valuable source of our relationship with him, our dreams?

The Bible tells of people who had high regard for God's communication in the form of dreams. Consider Daniel, a man of high esteem according to the words of an angel from the throne of God, and a dreamer renowned for his ability to interpret dreams. Or, read about Joseph, a dreamer of the Old Testament, as he moves from prison to being second in authority over all of Egypt, saving the nation of Israel (Gn 37–50) by bringing them to Egypt and thereby our hope of salvation. It is also interesting that another Joseph, a dreamer of the New Testament, saved God's son by bringing him to Egypt (Mt 1–2). Today, have we lost that former regard for dreams? Has the New Age movement and others picked up what we have discarded? Is it time we, the Church, take back what is rightfully ours? We think it is time for the Church to wake up to the possibility that our dreams can contain messages from God.

This book has four objectives:

1. *To show that God speaks to us through some of our dreams and through visions.* The prophet Joel[1] talks about more than just an outpouring of the Holy Spirit. He reports

some of the results of that outpouring—prophecy, dreams, and visions. Prophecy, one of the gifts of the Spirit, is a topic that has been amply dealt with by other writers. Dreams and visions, however, have had little attention.

2. *To awaken esteem for this wasted source of communication and relationship with God.* Dreams are mentioned throughout the Bible, and the people of the Bible had high regard for dreams. Many pivotal events in history have involved dreams, such as the birth and protection of the son of God. By exploring Scripture, we want to awaken an understanding of God's heart for dreams and the value he places on dreams. This will challenge us to wake up to this wasted source of relationship with our Father.

3. *To provide principles and insights to help Christians better understand dreams and their place in our lives and in the Church.* We believe that Christians and leaders need to be proactive in preparing for what will surely come in the last days. We find that the Church is interested in the outpouring of the Holy Spirit described in the prophecy of Joel 2:28. With this outpouring will come an increase in the experience of dreams and visions.

Therefore, we will provide ways of understanding the imagery and symbolism that often comprise dreams (and visions) so that the Church can be ready not only to walk that path themselves but also to guide anyone the Lord would bring to them with gentleness, understanding, and a listening informed heart.

4. *To demonstrate how God is using dreams in the counseling ministry to effect healing of emotions and memories.* As pastoral counselors, we are excited to find that God is speaking to his people through dreams to bring release from

those issues that imprison us and damage our relationships. This new and unique approach to counseling will be introduced in our book.

This book is written jointly by us both. When one of us makes a personal statement, we have added the name of the person in parentheses.

The dream is a communication gift from God that draws us closer to him, builds the Church, and edifies ourselves. Let us learn the skills needed to hear and understand as he speaks to us.

Steve and Dianne Bydeley, 2002

Part I

Background...

My people are destroyed for lack of knowledge.

Hosea 4:6

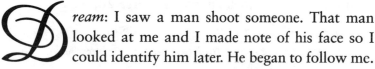

Chapter One

God Speaks

---

ream: I saw a man shoot someone. That man looked at me and I made note of his face so I could identify him later. He began to follow me.

Wherever I went, he followed. Over things, under, around, and through, he followed me. I went through a door and found myself in a small room. Others were there and they were all standing. There was no other door out. The man followed me into the room, blocking my escape. We stared at each other and then he started to move toward me. Suddenly, another man in the room grabbed him by the neck and picked him up off the floor. The stalker went completely limp and was totally helpless in the hands of this stranger.

Did you ever wake up from a dream like that and ask yourself what it was all about? *Who was the gunman that started to stalk me? Was Jesus the wonderful strong man who came to my rescue? What do I do with a dream like that? Was it something I ate? Was the dream supposed to be an encouragement?*

Do you dream? If you think you do not, or you cannot recall your dreams, there may be reasons for that. If you do dream—and I believe the evidence suggests we all do on occasion—you, too, have wondered about the creativity of the dream and its symbols. You, too, have wondered about its meaning, purpose, and origin. Some of these dreams may be more than the food we ate the night before or the result of a very active day.

In the book of Joel, chapter 2, verse 28, we read:

And afterward, I will pour out my Spirit on all people. Your sons and daughters will prophesy, your old men will dream dreams, your young men will see visions (NIV).

As the Church, we are very excited about the outpouring of the Holy Spirit in the latter days. In Acts 2, Peter declared this outpouring had begun and most today believe we are in those latter days and this outpouring is happening around the world. If this is true, what do we believe about the dreams and visions mentioned in this Scripture? Dreams and visions will be an important part of the latter-day outpouring, as John L. Sandford

Dreams and visions are an important part of the latter-day outpouring.

points out: "Dreams are one of the primary consequences of the outpouring of the Holy Spirit."[2] They are a *result* of the presence of the Holy Spirit on humankind, and they are important to the life and growth of the Church in these days. Are we equipping the Church, the body of Christ, to handle *every* facet of this outpouring or only that portion with which we are comfortable? What is it about dreams and visions that makes us uncomfortable? Are we afraid of hearing from God as were the Israelites of Exodus 20:18–19?

> *All the people perceived the thunder and the lightning flashes and the sound of the trumpet and the mountain smoking; and when the people saw it, they trembled and stood at a distance. Then they said to Moses, "Speak to us yourself and we will listen; but let not God speak to us, or we will die."*

God, at that time, presented himself as the law-giver, and he had just given the law to Moses and Aaron in the presence of the people. Today, this same God speaks to us through his son, Jesus, not in commandments but in grace, in mercy, in love, because Jesus fulfilled the demands of those commandments in his life, death, burial, and resurrection. Yes, we are expected to walk in harmony with the law, but even that requirement is being worked in us by his Holy Spirit. When he speaks to us today, it is as our Father, because not only were we saved from the consequences of our sin, he also adopted us to be his sons and daughters with all the rights and privileges due his children. He brought us into relationship with himself so he can walk with us, fellowship with us, have relationship with us, and speak with us, even perhaps through the pictures, images, and symbols of dreams or visions.

A Thousand Words

How does God speak to us today? Psalm 8:1 tells us:

O Lord, our Lord,
How majestic is Your name in all the earth,
Who have displayed Your splendor above the heavens!

How does "all the earth" display God's splendor? Have you studied the beauty of a rose, witnessed the flight of a hummingbird as it drinks nectar from a flower, or observed the dance and song of a whale and its calf in the ocean?

These and millions of other scenes like them are the echoes of God's creative acts in the beginning. These pictures declare the awesome majesty and glory of our God. They declare it even if no one will listen. They are pictures of the Godhead. Nature speaks to us of God in a language of pictures—the same kind of language that makes up our dreams and visions. It is not a difficult language; it is a language we can learn, a language of pictures and a picture is worth a thousand words.

Silence or Censorship

God, our Father, has spoken to humankind in various ways, including dreams and visions, throughout recorded history and still does today. From early in Genesis to the end of Revelation, he has shown himself to be a speaking God.

The Israelites were reminded of their promise to walk in God's ways, keep his statues, commandments, ordinances, and to "listen to His voice."[3]

God created us for relationship, with him and with those around us. The Ten Commandments, mentioned earlier, and all of the details of Moses' law are relationship issues. Jesus summarized all their demands:

> *And He said to him, "'YOU SHALL LOVE THE LORD YOUR GOD WITH ALL YOUR HEART, AND WITH ALL YOUR SOUL, AND WITH ALL YOUR MIND.' This is the great and foremost commandment. And a second is like it, 'YOU SHALL LOVE YOUR NEIGHBOR AS YOURSELF.' On these two commandments depend the whole Law and the Prophets* (Mt 22:37–40).

Communication—fresh communication—is a very important part of any relationship. An occasional phone call enhances the effect of the letters received, as anyone in a long-distance relationship knows. Letters and calls can sustain us until we can be together in relationship.

Paul admonishes us, in 1 Thessalonians 5:17, to "pray without ceasing." Prayer is dialogue, two-way communication, not the one-way communication of a monologue. We ask him, he answers us. He speaks to us, we respond to him. Of course, we hope for an answer or a response when we pray. God has things to say and there are things we sometimes need to hear, even though we may not have asked a question.

Jesus said, "my sheep know my voice"[4]—communication. He wants to communicate, to encourage, to advise, and to ask us to do things for him. Is that shepherd's voice calling to us, directing us to drink from the still water over there, to graze or rest here, stay away from that, or to follow as he leads perhaps in a different direction or to a new pasture?

In John 16:13, we read Jesus' words:

But when He, the Spirit of truth, comes, He will guide you into all the truth; for He will not speak on His own initiative, but whatever He hears, He will speak; and He will disclose to you what is to come.

"He will speak." The Greek word here is *laleo* which refers to speech, to using the tongue. It is also interesting that the root word from which *laleo* is derived is *lalos*, which means "talkative." Does that give a picture of relationship and communion?

The Outpouring

Through the prophet Joel, God says:

I will pour out My Spirit on all mankind; And your sons and daughters will prophesy, Your old men will dream dreams, Your young men will see visions (Jl 2:28).

This verse can be understood to read: "I will pour my Spirit on all mankind; and I will cause your sons and daughters to prophesy; I will cause your old men to dream dreams; I will cause your young men to see visions."

Thoughts of this outpouring bring to mind the difficulties Paul had to respond to in the Corinthian church regarding their enthusiasm for the gifts of the Spirit. The members there had to be instructed (guided, taught) in the orderly use and function of the gifts within the church body. The same may be the case regarding dreams in the Church today. Never did he suggest they not use the gifts, in fact, he admonished them to "eagerly desire spiritual gifts."[5]

We are aware of the problems and difficulties local churches may—and probably will—face as "new babes" learn to walk in this area of dreams and visions. Is it much different from the understanding parents have when their baby determines to walk? We know of the lumps and bruises we will have to rub and kiss better. We know they will trip and fall many times. We know they may hit their chins and bleed as new teeth cut their gums. Things will be knocked over and broken. There will be new conflicts with siblings as babies begin to roam. We know these trials are a part of the process of learning to walk, so we stand with them, we watch, we prepare ourselves to catch them if we can or to pick them up when we cannot. We are ready to help when it is necessary—and it will be necessary—because they must learn to walk. We would never forbid them to walk! Knowing that these things may happen in the Church, too, do we avoid talking about dreams, or do we ready ourselves to help?

It may be time for the Church to wake up... to dreams and visions!

Chapter Two

Defining Dreams and Visions

*I*f we are to wake up to dreams and visions, we need to lay some groundwork on the biblical use of these words. The Appendix of this book, on page 203, provides a "Key Words Study." That section lists the words used in the Old and New Testaments connected with dreams and visions. Please review this section and note how the various words are defined and used in Scripture. As we list verses in the rest of this book, we will include the Hebrew or Greek transliterations that apply in these verses. This will make it easy to relate the word to its meaning in the Key Words section.

Dreams

The obvious first word to look at is "dream." The Bible devotes no chapters or verses on the ceremonial procedures of dreaming, nothing on accepted postures for dreaming, nothing on how to dream. Dreams just happen, mostly at night but always when we are asleep. They are, for the most part, out of our control.

Researchers have found that dreams occur during the REM (Rapid Eye Movement) phase of Alpha sleep and these periods increase in length through the night with breaks between. Dreaming seems to be important to our physical and emotional well-being, as some researchers have concluded that even a few days without passing through the dream phase of sleep *would* lead to a major mental breakdown.[6] We may not remember all of our dreams, but we do dream—we must dream.

The *Encyclopedia Britannica* defines dreaming as follows:

> ...a hallucinatory experience that occurs during sleep. Dreaming, a common and distinctive phenomenon of sleep, has since the dawn of human history given rise to myriad beliefs, fears, and conjectures, both imaginative and experimental, regarding its mysterious nature. While any effort toward classification must be subject to inadequacies, beliefs about dreams fall into various classifications depending upon whether dreams are held to be reflections of reality, sources of divination, curative experiences, or evidence of unconscious activity.[7]

The dream, as suggested above, is a natural by-product of sleep. For his own reason, God has created us to need the dream process while we sleep for our emotional and physical well-being—a process into which God steps, at times, to communicate with us. We will see later that not all dreams are a direct communication from God.

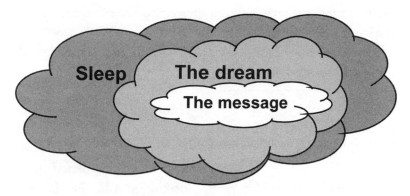

Some people claim not to dream or perhaps, more accurately, they do not remember their dreams. This is common when dreams are the result of natural processes. However, message dreams are important to remember and retain. In chapter 5, "Practical Dreaming," we have listed some thoughts and actions to help the dream process for those who think they do not dream or have difficulty remembering their dreams in the morning.

> Message dreams are a sequence of images, symbols, sounds, and emotions with meaning, clarity, and purpose.

In summary then, message dreams are a sequence of images, symbols, sounds, and emotions with meaning, clarity, and purpose that come to us through the agency of sleep. In the chapters that follow, we will examine a framework for understanding these images, symbols, sounds, and emotions.

Visions

Vision: I (Steve) was looking down on a city cloaked in darkness. In the middle of the city I saw a tall, triangular building. On the roof of this building I saw a silly grin smiling at me. I then turned to see a platter being presented to me. On the platter was a pair of socks with Christian symbols on them. I turned back to look at the city but it was no longer there and I found myself looking at a wall in my home.

> Visions come as a more direct intrusion into the moment of the day through the agency of a trance.

The meaning of this vision eluded me for many days—until I was in Canberra, the capital city of Australia. I happened to be looking at a banner fluttering in the breeze, when suddenly I saw the triangular building with that smile. That image represented the center of the city of Canberra. Designed into the layout of the city is the Freemasons' divider and square. The parliament building is situated at the apex of the divider, two main streets are the legs of the divider (the triangular building in my dream), and the lakes (in my dream the silly-looking grin) represent the square. The socks may indicate that God made it possible for us to sneak into the city (in our socks) under the guise of a tour but with authority (the Christian symbols) to pray over the city from Mount Ainslie, a high point (as in the dream). This we did on the second evening of our visit to that city. The next day we were able to tour the inside of the parliament building to a degree that has been allowed only once before in its history. There may be more yet to understand concerning the socks.

Visions are similar to dreams. They, too, are a sequence of images, symbols, sounds, and emotions with meaning, clarity, and purpose. These images come by day or night as a vision by way of a trance as a more direct intrusion into a moment of time while we are awake. Scripture uses the terms together in the following verses:

He flies away like a dream [chalom], *and they cannot find him; Even like a vision* [chizzayon] *of the night he is chased away* (Jb 20:8).

And the multitude of all the nations who wage war against Ariel, Even all who wage war against her and her stronghold, and who distress her, Shall be like a dream [chalom], *a vision* [chazown] *of the night* (Is 29:7).

...a vision [horama] *appeared to Paul in the night: a certain man of Macedonia was standing and appealing to him, and saying, "Come over to Macedonia and help us"* (Acts 16:9).

Visions come to us through the agency of a trance in the same way as dreams come to us through the agency of sleep. The trance can be defined as "a half-conscious state characterized by an absence of response to external stimuli."[8]

The word *trance* is used in the New Testament but today seems to have a negative stigma associated with it; therefore, we prefer to suggest that visions come as a more direct intrusion into our space-time continuum.

This agency for the communication of visions has been recorded twice in the New Testament.[9] In both of these instances, the person went into a trance and saw a vision.

The Bible, in these verses, mentions the trance as a method God used to enable one to receive a vision. Peter's account refers to the vision he received in later verses.[10] Paul's account tells that he fell into a trance and *saw* Jesus. The trance must be God-induced. Many other religious groups will induce a trance by "meditation, biofeedback, hypnosis, and drug-induced states"[11] to enable an individual to receive communication from spirits around them or those thought to be their ancestors. These inducement types, we believe, can open one to the very real realm and influence of the demonic—a situation best avoided. When the trance is God's doing, there is protection from all unwanted influences.

The trance is only the agency through which the vision comes in the same way sleep is the agency through which dreams come. We will soon examine principles for understanding the images and symbols of visions that are the same as those for dreams.

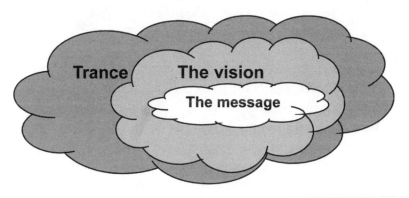

In summary, then, visions are a sequence of images, symbols, sounds, and emotions with meaning, clarity, and purpose that come to us through the agency of a trance.

Pictures

Frequently, during prayer for others, a person may receive a message in the form of a picture in their mind. Some consider this a vision while others see it as a prophetic message. In either case, these pictures may be approached in the same manner as dreams and visions.

Conclusion

For simplicity, we will refer generally to dreams because they seem to be more common, although, for the occasional illustration, we will use a vision to draw attention to some aspect or to draw conclusions. Messages that come to us as dreams or as visions are similar as are the principles that apply to them. Both are sequences of images, symbols, sounds, and emotions with meaning, clarity, and purpose. These messages can come at night as a dream during sleep or by day or night as a vision. The Bible gives us examples when, for urgency, the message of the dream or vision did not come as imagery but by direct verbal instruction. In those cases, interpretation was not necessary—only immediate action.

Clarifying the terms for dreams and visions may be inconsequential if we have little or no regard for dreams as a part of our life. Dreams have, in fact, lost a great deal of their former respect for reasons we hope to challenge in the following chapters.

Chapter Three

The Demise of Dreams

As you read the Old Testament, it is evident that some people had very high regard for dreams and a strong interest in understanding their meaning. One of these, a king, had a dream and, when he woke in the morning, we suspect he could not remember it. This can be very frustrating when you are serious about your dreams, but, being a king, he had a solution.

> *The king answered and said to the Chaldeans, "The command from me is firm: if you do not make known to me the dream* [chelem] *and its interpretation, you will be torn limb from limb, and your houses will be made a rubbish heap"* (Dn 2:5).

It seems very clear that the king was serious about understanding this dream. What changed our perspective on dreams? Why has our esteem for dreams fallen to the very low levels we experience today?

Strategies of the Enemy

The strength of any army relies on the unity of their purpose, strategy, and effort. The Roman armies were known for a particular strategy—divide and conquer. By dividing the opposing army into small groups that lacked unity, it was easier to systematically conquer the smaller groups. Modern military strategy still works in the same way.

It has been interesting to witness the strategies of modern armies in conflict these last few years. We have seen two conflicts—named "Operation Desert Storm" against Iraq and the "War Against Terror" in Afghanistan—in particular. As we have watched the coverage, as it unfolded halfway around the world, among the first objectives of the attack was to disrupt and/or destroy the communication network of the enemy as we read in a CNN update on the "War Against Terror":

> Defense Secretary Donald Rumsfeld and Gen. Richard Myers, chairman of the Joint Chiefs of Staff, said the attacks sought to take out more of the Taliban's command and control assets, to cut off their communications and hamper their ability to mount coordinated military operations.[12]

Why is the destruction of communications such a high priority in a military conflict? Divide and conquer.

By destroying the communications systems of your opponent, you destroy their unity, cohesion, and their connection to potential support. Rather than face a large army unified by the ability to communicate with a central command post, you now face smaller pockets of resistance with different objectives—often their own immediate needs. Thus, using precision bombs and laser-guided missiles, the network of communication towers and radio and television broadcasting stations of the enemy were destroyed. The result left pockets of enemy forces throughout the country, all prepared to fight but without a unifying leadership. This reduced the battle to smaller conflicts to be fought only when it became convenient or necessary.

We, too, have an enemy against whom we struggle:

> *For our struggle is not against flesh and blood, but against the rulers, against the powers, against the world forces of this darkness, against the spiritual forces of wickedness in the heavenly places* (Eph 6:12).

Toward the Church, the whole body of Christ, this enemy may have the same objective and strategy. By disrupting, destroying, or discrediting the communication systems within the body, we become many little pockets of believers without the ability to receive directives from our central command—the Lord Jesus Christ. Our enemy has been able to reduce our concerted effort to little, tolerable pockets of resistance. All around the world today we have little pockets of resistance with no unified effort. We *need* to reestablish our communication systems!

One of our longstanding means of communication with God has been dreams and visions. Throughout the Bible, from Genesis to Revelation, God has spoken to his people through dreams and visions. Not only have these played an important role in the past, God has promised to continue to do so in the last days.

> *And afterward, I will pour out my Spirit on all people. Your sons and daughters will prophesy, your old men will dream dreams, your young men will see visions* (Jl 2:28, NIV).

This prophecy was used by Peter[13] to explain to those around what had happened to the 120 disciples gathered in the upper room in Jerusalem. His words were, *"...this is what was spoken of through the prophet Joel"* (Acts 2:16).

It was this outpouring of the Holy Spirit that the prophet, Joel, was referring to; it happened and has been happening since the day of Pentecost. What can we expect to see happen when the Holy Spirit is poured out on all humankind?

- Your offspring will prophesy;
- Your young people will see visions;
- Your older people will dream dreams.

There seems to be something for everyone. These things are the immediate result of the Holy Spirit coming into the lives of God's people, his army, the citizens of his Kingdom.

How does this become our communication method with central command? We read in John 16:13:

> But when He, the Spirit of truth, comes, He will guide you into all the truth; for He will not speak on His own initiative, but whatever He hears, He will speak; and He will disclose to you what is to come.

There are other verses that inform us of the things the Holy Spirit does as a result of being poured out. He will guide you and disclose to you the things that are to come. This may include battle strategies.

How will he disclose and guide us? The Bible does play a major role, but the Bible was not able to tell Peter to go and share the gospel message with the gentiles in Caesarea. Nor could the Bible have directed Paul to go to Macedonia on the next leg of his travels. Nor could it have told Joseph that it was okay for him to take Mary as his wife.

We need up-to-date instruction and directives. No battle can be won by following the commands and directives that were issued a month or a year ago. They need to be fresh and current to be effective or, better yet, to come in advance of the enemy's plans.[14]

Our enemy has been very effective in destroying and discrediting dreams and visions as a method of communicating with our Commander-in-Chief. Too many of us have been left to divine, presume, or guess God's will and direction for our lives and our churches. Who can know the mind of God except the Spirit of God? *"...the thoughts of God no one knows except the Spirit of God"* (1 Cor 2:11).

Do we want to be an effective force in this world? Do we want to be a unified strength affecting the people of this world? We need to be in touch with the mind and thoughts of God. We need to hear his directives, his marching orders. We need to learn to use the communication systems of our Kingdom. We need to teach the soldiers under our command how to receive communications and instructions. And we need to obey the directives we receive. Only then will we become a unified people under the leadership of our Commander-in-Chief, Jesus Christ.

The following are some factors that show how our regard for dreams has been destroyed.

Factors in the Demise

Science

Science has had a profound effect on our regard for dreams. Much of our science is rooted in the Greek thinking of men like Plato, Aristotle, and Hippocrates. Plato (427–347 BC) taught that human beings could gain knowledge from three sources: reason, their five senses, and spiritual sources. He had regard for the spiritual dimension, but thinkers thereafter became increasingly humanistic. For example, Aristotle (384–322 BC), a pupil of Plato, taught that senses and reason were the only means by which we acquire knowledge. Hippocrates (460–377 BC), the founder of modern medicine, saw dreams as merely a bodily process. The decay in the esteem for dreams is evident.

The World

The Age of Enlightenment is a phrase used to describe a time around the 1800s when anything that science and logical thinking could not explain tended to be rejected by society. Many believe this movement was a reaction against the control the Church exercised over the minds and actions of people. Unfortunately, reaction to anything often swings too far in the opposite direction. Enlightened society stripped the Church of its influence and turned instead to reason (logical thinking) and the senses. Today, rationalism fights to maintain control of our minds or, more accurately, is the facade in this fight and not our real enemy as we read earlier (Eph 6:12).

Sigmund Freud

Freud (1856–1939), a physician and the founder of modern psychoanalysis, suggested that dreams are the product of unconscious conflicts in childhood sexual drives and impulses. An adult person with a mature mind and the help of an analyst could recognize and resolve these conflicts where the young mind could not.

Carl Jung

Jung (1875–1961), a Swiss psychiatrist and founder of analytical psychology, suggested that dreams were the result of unconscious emotional conflicts caused by an imbalance in their male-female natures (*animus/anima*). He also taught that animals in dreams represented our unresolved emotional conflicts. Dreams were regarded as a naturalistic process.

> This new knowledge of the biology of dreaming does not suggest that dreams have no meaning. Dreams are meaningful mental products just as thoughts and daydreams are. They express important wishes, fears, concerns, and worries of the dreamer so the study and analysis of dreams can often be a useful procedure, revealing different aspects of a person's mental functions.[15]

The New Age

The many-faceted New Age movement unrestrainedly embraces dreams as a form of communication with the higher consciousness and/or guiding spirits. Visiting the New Age section of any secular bookstore presents convincing evidence of this. Does the fact that New Age followers have embraced "dream stuff" mean that the Church should avoid the issue? We appear to have abandoned the rainbow—God's sign of a covenant with humankind—to New Age adherents. Should we abandon dreams to them as well?

Cultural Attitudes

Our culture reflects our current attitude toward dreams through phrases like "in your dreams" or "dream on" and others that degrade our esteem for dreams. How often have you been told, "It's okay now; you were only dreaming," or "Forget it; it was only a dream"? These phrases are an indication of how little regard we have for dreams. Some of this low regard comes from our ignorance and impatience in working through dream language.

The Church

When have you heard a sermon on dreams and dreaming? How many Bible colleges offer a course on the interpretation of dreams?

What happened to dreams within the Church? Herman Riffel writes:

> Another damaging influence against observing the messages of dreams came through a serious mistranslation of one word by Jerome in the Latin Vulgate. In Deuteronomy 18:10, Leviticus 19:26 and 2 Chronicles 33:6 we are told not to practice witchcraft. Jerome translated the Hebrew word for "witchcraft" as dreams. From that serious mistranslation the teaching that we are not to observe the message of dreams was carried over into the Roman Catholic Church, which had a great influence on the Church as a whole.[16]

This mistranslation would have directed Church leaders to forbid any practice dealing with dreams. The consequences of giving attention to dreams would be the same as those associated with witchcraft:

> *For whoever does these things is detestable to the* LORD; *and because of these detestable things the* LORD *your God will drive them out before you* (Dt 18:12).

Regard for dreams has succumbed to the secular world view because psychology teaches that they are just a natural human psychological process. There is, therefore, nothing supernatural or spiritual about them.

The Church has been swayed to believe that human psychology and things to do with dreams are much too difficult for the unlearned to comprehend. It is best left to those who have studied long and hard—the "professionals."

The Church should reclaim this area of ministry.

Conclusion

Is it any wonder we have such low esteem for dreams? Yet, when we wake up from a vivid dream, we are left with a fascination, a curiosity, and a feeling there must be a meaning or a message in that dream. In spite of low regard for dreams, we have an interest, deep down, in understanding our dreams. The first step in satisfying our curiosity is rebuilding our regard for dreams.

Chapter Four

Rebuilding Our Regard for Dreams

Our low esteem for dreams, as discussed in the previous chapter, should have been no surprise to us. It has been part of our way of life for many years. We want to reverse that trend now and encourage and excite you to the prospects of hearing from God in a more personal way in your everyday walk with him. Let me give you an example.

Dream: I was traveling and came to the motel. As I entered my room, I noticed that five drinking glasses had been arranged in a circle. I recognized it to be a symbol of a witch's coven. After moving the glasses to break the circle, I prayed through the room, cleansing it of any defilement.

In the days prior to that dream, we had been traveling and, on two occasions, I (Steve) was suddenly overcome with a fever. The next morning, the fever was gone but it returned in the evening. This happen twice at different motels and it had our attention. We have a practice of "praying through" motel rooms when we arrive because of what may have occurred in those rooms by past occupants. John L. Sandford writes:

> A missionary returning from the Far East informed me that it had become common for a Chinese family going on a trip to ask a Christian family to come and live in their home while they were away, especially if there had been a death in the family. They knew that when they returned, their home would again possess a clean, wholesome atmosphere because of the prayers of the Christians.[17]

My dream reminded us of the importance not only of praying through the room on entry but also after the room had been cleaned (the five glasses). We have never found five glasses in any room, but in the dream they represented the daily room service. We immediately made changes to our daily routine in response to the message of that dream and had no further problems. Did the problem stop because we responded to the message of the dream?

We have a high regard for our dreams and this has increased as we have grown in our awareness that God does speak to us through dreams.

What are some of the most compelling references in the Bible to hearing from God through dreams today? The most compelling may be one quoted already from Joel 2:28.

The direct effect of the Holy Spirit being poured out onto all people will be that we will prophesy, dream dreams, and see visions. Jesus tells us that, when the Holy Spirit comes, he will speak what he hears, tell us of future events, and make known to us those things that belong to Jesus and to the Father.

> *But when he, the Spirit of truth, comes, he will guide you into all truth. He will not speak on his own; he will speak only what he hears, and he will tell you what is yet to come* (Jn 16:13 NIV).

It is time to raise our regard for dreams and prepare ourselves to hear what the Spirit says to us and to the Church through us. Could it be that, in his heart, God wants to do more for us in our faith walk, our sanctification, and our healing? Is it his heart's desire to be in closer relationship with us than we have been aware of or even imagined until now?

We want to raise our regard for dreams in this chapter by looking at how God has used dreams throughout biblical history in very important and strategic ways.

God's Teaching on Dreams in the Bible

The Bible is our primary method for knowing God, his ways, and his truth. It is not just a history book; it is living, and active.

> *For the word of God is living and active and sharper than any two-edged sword, and piercing as far as the division of soul and spirit, of both joints and marrow, and able to judge the thoughts and intentions of the heart* (Heb 4:12).

The Bible is the standard against which we evaluate our thoughts and intentions. It also is the standard against which we affirm the correctness of the interpretation of our dreams and our response to those dreams. The first step we will take is to see what God says to us about dreams and visions in the Bible. Then we will look at some of the Bible's dreams and show how God used them and their timing in significant ways and how the recipients of dreams responded to their message.

What does God tell us about dreams in the Bible?

> *He said, "Hear now My words: If there is a prophet among you, I, the* LORD, *shall make Myself known to him in a vision* [marah]. *I shall speak with him in a dream* [chalom]" (Nm 12:6).

> *...it will come about after this That I will pour out My Spirit on all mankind; And your sons and daughters will prophesy, Your old men will dream* [chalam] *dreams* [chalom], *Your young men will see visions* [chizzayon] (Jl 2:28).

The Bible is truth; it tells us to expect dreams and visions (referred to collectively as dreams) because of the Holy Spirit in our lives, and it tells us that he will speak to us through dreams. A large portion of the Bible comes to us as the result of dreams and visions. Often our dreams come from God. We believe that God, our Father, gives us these dreams for a purpose and that he wants us to understand the message of the dream.

Dreams of the Bible

When we see how much of the Bible deals with dreams and visions we should gain appreciation for God's high regard for dreams. Our understanding of eschatology (the doctrine of end times) comes almost entirely from information revealed through dreams and visions. We cannot understand today's news reports about the events in the Middle East unless we have a firm grasp of the book of Genesis, a book in which dreams play a commendable role.

We believe that being familiar with the dreams of the Bible will give us much insight into God's use of dream language. Follow as we examine a few examples of those dreams.

Genesis 37:5–10

Joseph had two similar dreams. In the first dream, this farm boy saw the sheaf of grain he had tied stand erect and the sheaves his brothers had tied circling and bowing to his. In the second dream, Joseph saw the sun, the moon, and eleven stars bowing down to him. In both dreams, the sheaves and the stars were very common and personal to his lifestyle and experience.

We suspect Joseph may not have known the meaning or significance of these dreams. However, his brothers and father knew immediately what they meant. The brothers had some regard for dreams because, after hearing them, they hated Joseph even more. They may have interpreted the dreams to foretell Joseph receiving a large portion of the family inheritance as Jacob's favored son. Whatever the case, Joseph's apparent death would end any possibility for the fulfillment of those dreams and selling him as a slave would make bowing to him an unlikely event—or would it? Even though Jacob was indignant toward Joseph regarding the second dream, he kept the words of the dream in his heart[18]—as did Joseph—for many years.[19]

Those dreams came true exactly as they had been interpreted, although it took some twenty years to happen. Timing is important for us to remember when we are tempted to expect instant fulfillment of our dreams. Did God plant those words in Joseph's heart so they could work faith and sustain him through many years in prison?

Genesis 40:5–8

Pharaoh threw his baker and cupbearer into prison for offending him, and both were worried at the outcome of the impending investigation. One night, each had a dream. They soon learned that one of the other prisoners was gifted in understanding dreams, so they approached him. Although somewhat similar, the dreams had different meanings. Each dream had symbolism that was personal to the dreamer: the baker dreamt of bread in baskets and the cupbearer, of squeezing grapes into a cup. Three vines and three baskets represented three days. The birds' eating the bread was a bad symbol for the baker. In the end, the cupbearer was restored to office and the baker was executed, just as Joseph had interpreted. In both dreams, the dreamer was active in the dream. This, we will learn, is a subjective dream—about and for the dreamer.

After some twenty years as a slave and in prison, Joseph had gained some insight into dreams. Perhaps there was little else to do at times. He considered dreams important and recognized their source to be God.[20] God set the stage for Joseph's influence on the world with those dreams.

Genesis 41:1–8

It was the Pharaoh's turn to dream and he had two. In the first dream, seven healthy, fat cows came out of the Nile and were followed by seven thin, ugly cows. The seven ugly, thin cows ate the seven healthy, fat cows, and they remained thin and ugly afterward. In the second dream, seven thin, dry ears of grain ate seven juicy ears of grain, and they, too, remained thin and dry. He summoned all his wise men; no one could understand the dreams. The cup-bearer then remembered his dream and his two-year-old promise and told Pharaoh who summoned Joseph to help.

Joseph then answered Pharaoh, saying, "It is not in me; God will give Pharaoh a favorable answer" (Gn 41:16).

Pharaoh, no doubt a man of commerce and familiar with cattle and grain, was troubled by the bottom line of his dreams—a poor return on investment. He needed answers, and God had already been actively making Joseph ready for this time with those answers. The two dreams—a repetition—meant the outcome was assured. The seven fat and seven thin represented two seven-year periods, lush and lean respectively.

We know the outcome of these dreams was important for the survival of the Hebrews. In the dreams, Pharaoh stood on the bank of the Nile River. He was an observer of the events in the dream. He was not involved in the dream except to watch. The dream was not about him—it was an objective dream. The setting was not just a river; it was the Nile River, central to Egypt. Provision came from the Nile. The east wind was pictured as dry and scorching—from the desert. The draught came from the east wind. You know the outcome of those dreams.[21] Have you ever wondered what the outcome would have been had anyone other than Pharaoh had received that dream? Would Pharaoh have responded as decisively to the message as he did?

God used those two dreams in a way crucial to the survival of Israel and eventually for the coming of the promised Messiah.

Judges 7:13–15

The Lord used a dream in a different way: he gave this dream to a Midian soldier, an enemy of Israel. The dream showed a barley loaf tumbling into the camp of Midian, hitting a tent, and knocking it flat. Barley was the grain of poor people and often used as animal feed as well. Gideon's army may have considered itself as animal feed in comparison to the size of the enemy's army. The picture is one of a small loaf of bread that knocked down a large tent designed to withstand the high winds of the desert environment. A picture of absurdity—very much like Gideon's army of 300 men attacking the tens of thousands of the enemy using clay pots and torches. We read in these verses that the Midianite who received the dream understood it and related its meaning to a colleague while Gideon was listening.

The Lord asked Gideon to reduce his army. When Gideon finished he had reduced his army from 32,000 men to only 300 to fight against the innumerable Midianite and Amalekite armies. The purpose in reducing Gideon's army to 300 was so everyone would know it was not in their own strength they won the battle. God used a dream given to the enemy to encourage Gideon's army. They were victorious because the Lord fought the fight. God gave this dream to the Midianite in a way that allowed Gideon to hear the dream and the dreamer's interpretation of it. The result was significant in encouraging Gideon and his army in a logistically absurd situation.

Daniel 7

Daniel had a dream that was full of terrifying images. He was diligent in writing down the dream. The dream was of the four winds of heaven blowing, stirring up the sea; four creatures came out of the sea, each one different. The first was like a lion with wings like an eagle. As he watched, the wings were plucked and it was made to stand like a man. The second creature resembled a bear with three ribs in its teeth. The third beast was like a leopard with four heads and four wings. This beast was given authority. Finally the last creature came. It was dreadful looking with iron teeth and ten horns; it was strong and boastful. The dream told of the horns and of one horn with eyes like a man and mouth full of boasting. As Daniel watched, he described the "Ancient of Days" seated on the throne with a river flowing out from him. Books were opened. This last creature, the boastful one, was slain and thrown into burning fire. The other beasts were given a longer time to live. Then the Son of Man came to take dominion of his kingdom, one that will never pass away.

What an amazing dream for that period! Notice Daniel's role in the dream was that of an observer. This is an indication that the dream was not likely to be about Daniel; it was an objective dream. The characteristics of the animals represent the characteristics of future kings and their nations. The dream has such clarity and understanding for us, today, but it was not so clear for Daniel. This, too, is a characteristic of an objective dream: the symbols may not be familiar to the dreamer if the dream is for someone else or, as in this case, those in the future. Read these verses again in different versions of the Bible and try to imagine the alarm and distress Daniel felt. Did God entrust that dream and others like it to Daniel because he was diligent in recording and responding to them?

God's heart for dreams sometimes discloses future events so we do not have to walk in fear. As the events unfold, we can be assured God is in control. The first creatures, representing the kingdoms of the Medes/Persians and Greeks, very accurately described what happened in history after Daniel's time, but there remains yet the last creature to be revealed, undoubtedly with the same accuracy. Many have thrown their speculations onto the table for scrutiny and many more watch to see that last event unfold.

Matthew's Gospel

Take a moment and read the first two chapters of Matthew. Pay particular attention to each mention of dreams. You will find there that dreams directed the birth announcement, naming, life, and survival of God's son.

> *...an angel of the Lord appeared to him in a dream* [onar], *saying, "Joseph, son of David, do not be afraid to take Mary as your wife; for that which has been conceived in her is of the Holy Spirit. ...she will bear a Son; and you shall call His name Jesus..."* (Mt 1:20).

> *...having been warned by God in a dream* [onar] *not to return to Herod,* [the magi] *departed for their own country by another way* (Mt 2:12).

> *...an angel of the Lord appeared to Joseph in a dream* [onar], *saying, "Arise and take the Child and His mother, and flee to Egypt, and remain there until I tell you"* (Mt 2:13).

> *...an angel of the Lord appeared in a dream* [onar] *to Joseph in Egypt, saying, "Arise and take the Child and His mother, and go into the land of Israel"* (Mt 2:19–20).

And being warned by God in a dream [onar], *he departed for the regions of Galilee, and came and resided in a city called Nazareth* (Mt 2:22–23).

The Almighty God, creator of all things, the one who can undo all of creation with a single word, chose to use dreams to announce, protect, and guide the events related to the birth of his beloved son, Jesus. These dreams were unique in that they were without symbolism as told to us by Matthew. Given the urgency of the message, God needed to be direct.

Could he trust us with dreams like that today? Would we respond as obediently as did Joseph?

Acts 10:9–16

Peter's vision on the rooftop in Joppa was pivotal to the history of the Church. While they were cooking a meal, Peter fell into a trance and saw the vision. This was the vision in which Peter saw a sheet (also translated a sail and, therefore, a very personal symbol to the fisherman) full of unclean animals being lowered by four corners out of heaven. The voice in the dream told him to kill and eat. He refused because they were unclean animals. This same vision is repeated two more times. Then he heard a knock at the door and found a company of Gentiles had arrived suggesting God directed them to bring him to Caesarea. No, he does not kill and eat them! The message of the dream is in the sentence, "Do not call unclean what God has made clean" (v.15).

At this time and using this method, God indicated the message of the gospel was for the Gentiles as well as the Jews. When Peter delivered the gospel message, God confirmed his intentions by pouring out his Holy Spirit on those Gentiles[22] as he had on the Jews during Pentecost.[23]

Have you noticed that, many centuries earlier while in Joppa, the prophet Jonah was called by God to preach to the Gentiles in Nineveh? In this account, however, Jonah refused to go.

> *But Jonah… went down to Joppa, found a ship that was going to Tarshish, paid the fare, and went down into it to go with them to Tarshish from the presence of the* LORD *(Jonah 1:3).*

This time, also in Joppa, Simon Barjona (Mt 16:16), meaning son of Jonah, later renamed Peter, was asked to go and share the gospel with the Gentiles. Because of the vision of the unclean animals he went (unlike Jonah), curious to see what God was going to do for them. Would Peter have accompanied the Gentiles who, moments after the vision, knocked at the door, if he had not first had that vision?

We have to wonder what the Lord could do for the Church and for the unsaved if we were more diligent in recording and acting on the dreams he gives us.

> *Indeed, God speaks once, Or twice, yet no one notices it. In a dream* [chalom], *a vision* [chizzayon] *of the night, When sound sleep falls on men, While they slumber in their beds, Then He opens the ears of men, And seals their instruction* (Jb 33:14–16).

Lord, help us to notice, hear, and respond correctly to you knowing your heart for dreams.

A List of Bible Dreams and Visions

The following chart lists many of the dreams and visions of the Bible for review at your leisure.

Book	Chapters	Dreamer
Genesis	15	Abraham
	20	Abimelech
	28, 46	Jacob
	31	Jacob and Laban
	37	Joseph
	40	Cupbearer and Baker
	41	Pharaoh
Judges	7	Midianite soldier
1 Samuel	3	Samuel
2 Samuel	7	Nathan
1 Chronicles	17	Nathan
2 Chronicles	26	Zechariah
1 Kings	3	Solomon
Job	4	Eliphaz
Isaiah	1, 21, 22	Isaiah
Ezekiel	1, 8, 12, 43	Ezekiel
Daniel	2, 4	Nebuchadnezzar
	7, 8, 9, 10, 11	Daniel
Amos	1	Amos
Obadiah	1	Obadiah

Book	Chapters	Dreamer
Nahum	1	Nahum
Habakkuk	1	Habakkuk
Matthew	1	Joseph
	2	Joseph and Magi
	17	Peter, James and John
	27	Pilate's wife
Luke	1	Zacharias
	24	Women
Acts	9	Ananias
	10	Cornelius and Peter
	12	Peter
	16, 18	Paul
2 Corinthians	12	Paul
Revelation	1	John

Conclusion

We have looked at only a few of the dreams recorded in the Bible. We can see how people entrusted their lives to the outcome of these dreams, up to and including Jesus, the son of God. Their regard for dreams is obvious, as was their desire to hear from God. During King Saul's last days we read:

When Saul inquired of the LORD, the LORD did not answer him, either by dreams or by Urim or by prophets (1 Sm 28:6).

As we have studied a few of the dreams of the Bible, we have witnessed the regard their recipients had for dreams, consequently placing ourselves on the path of learning what to do with dreams, how to understand them, and how to respond to them. It is an interesting journey, as you will see.

Chapter Five

Practical Dreaming

*D*uring public presentations of this material, we have been asked questions that focus on some of the practical issues of dreaming. Questions come from those wanting to know how to get started, those who had not considered dreams important, many wanting to know how to give dreams a place of honor in their lives, and others who say they do not dream. This chapter is offered as an encouragement to those who have a desire to learn more and to grow in this area of relationship with God.

The following is a brief record of my process as I (Dianne) have grown in my understanding of dreams.

God Wants to Speak

While still a new Christian, I was told that God wanted to speak to me, a concept that fascinated me! When I learned that one of the ways he speaks to us is through dreams, I was intrigued because I often dreamt. This was about God, the creator of all life, his Spirit, and our Redeemer wanting to communicate with me. Dreams now offered a new perspective and relevance in my life. My anticipation and excitement were high as I launched into this new adventure. With all my heart, I wanted to hear from him.

I knew of no one who could guide me in this dream experience, but I wanted to learn, so my first step was to purchase a notebook which I placed beside my bed. Then I asked the Lord our God to speak and went to bed excited by what the night might bring.

Spirit-to-Spirit Connection

What I liked most about the concept of God communicating with me through dreams was that my conscious mind was out of the equation. When I am awake and hear God, my mind can influence my hearing by analyzing, intellectualizing, and theorizing—making every attempt to figure things out. In a dream, there is no opportunity to question or doubt, because God fashions the dream and I receive it. My mind, for the most part, is denied involvement making dreams a Spirit-to-spirit connection initiated by God.

> My mind, for the most part, is denied involvement, making dreams a Spirit-to-spirit connection initiated by him.

Recording Dreams

As this new determination to understand dreams began, I discovered it was most frustrating to have an exciting and significant dream in the night only to awaken in the morning with no memory of its details. Waking up in the night to record a dream was difficult, but, by doing so, I would at least have a record of it in the morning. At first I turned on the light to record my dream but soon realized this was less than ideal because the contrast between dark and light was too severe an adjustment for my eyes. The harshness of the light also affected my concentration on the details of the dream, so a search began for a better light. For a long time, I used a flashlight with my hand covering the lens to give a dull glow. Then I was given a pen with a built-in flashlight, but it, too, had to be modified being too bright. Recently, Steve found a small flashlight that has a mini lantern option that sits at the top of my page, casting a soft light for easy writing.

Some people dictate their dreams into a tape recorder, but to do so you must speak clearly or you may not understand your nighttime mumblings in the morning. If you dictate to tape, take the time the next day to write it out properly, clearly, and include any details of context (more on context in chapter 11). You will be amazed at the understanding that begins to come in the writing process. In Daniel 7:1, we read:

> *In the first year of Belshazzar king of Babylon Daniel saw a dream* [chelem] *and visions* [chezev] *in his mind as he lay on his bed; then he wrote the dream* [chelem] *down and related the following summary of it.*

Daniel understood that proper handling of a dream requires it be written down. We have the entire book of Daniel because he wrote down what he saw.

As a dream came, I woke and faithfully wrote it in my bedside exercise book. When writing the dream, it is important to do so without analysis—just the details of the dream. In the casual (non-analytical) writing of the dream, a feature or phrase would frequently catch my attention leading to a moment of understanding to even a small part of the dream.

Much persistence is required when recording dreams as it can take some two to ten minutes to record a dream, and, in having as many as six dreams some nights, it is easy to see how the interruption of sleep could take a toll on the next day. As tired as I was, I persisted in writing down my dreams, trusting God's grace would sustain me though the following day, and he indeed proved faithful.

Reasons for Recording Dreams

Over time, I have learned several important reasons for recording dreams.

- Writing them down in the night meant I could review them in the morning. As the morning dawned and my mind turned to the events of the day, I could seldom recall a dream had I not written it in the night.

- Writing and dating the dream not only gave me the big picture, it also enabled me to recall the details, the symbols, the flow, and the context.

- Understanding into the message of the dream frequently came as I wrote it out. A phrase, an image, a symbol, a color, an association of a person, or some other thing would leap off the page as I recorded the dream, leading to a full or partial moment of understanding.

- Often, understanding of the dream came in the midst of everyday life, days or weeks or even months later.

Reviewing past dreams can bring understanding where there have been common themes, symbols, or issues.

- Establishing a dream vocabulary comes by comparing the symbols, images, people, animals, etc., in various dreams from different seasons. This develops into understanding of the bigger picture of your dream vocabulary.

- Things the Lord has shown me about dreams can bless others. I have filled many notebooks with dreams, and it is interesting to see how the Lord is providing opportunities to share what I have learned. We pray others are blessed and encouraged as together we continue to learn.

- Take time to do an honorable job in keeping a record of your dreams out of respect for the Giver of the dream, for that is the task of a "good and faithful servant."

Frustrations

Now allow me to share that not all this dream stuff was a glorious experience. For about three years, as I recorded every dream, resentment and frustration grew because of the many dream fragments, dreams that seemed to go nowhere, "pizza dreams," and seeming nightmares. Why was God giving me all these dreams without the interpretations? I grew frustrated and, sadly, directed my frustration toward him. For years, I had little understanding of their meanings, and I had a longing to know what he was telling me but felt like he was speaking a foreign language. I grew increasingly discouraged because the understanding of my dreams was evading me.

Praying through Dreams

In the process, I was also learning that prayer was an important ingredient, so I woke early to have a forty-five-minute "tea-time" with God. I determined to take time to pray through the dreams of that night. I laugh now, remembering how, at 6 a.m., I was trying to read and pray through the symbols of the new dreams. When I had finished reading the dreams, I would look toward God and say, "So what now, God? I still don't understand anything." For many years, my prayers were weak and meager as I tried to understand the dream images and pictures. Often, before I could get through even one of several of that night's dreams, time would have slipped by and I would have to leave for work. The frustration continued because I still had such little understanding of their meaning. Having done all I could, I felt like quitting, not wanting to write down, work, or pray through another dream!

But somewhere deep inside, I remembered the original reason I had been excited about dreams. God wanted to communicate with me. I had to rest in his sovereignty, believing he was able to bring me to an understanding of everything I needed, so, in spite of the frustrations, I continued to record my dreams —with much less intensity. In the morning, I held up to him the dreams of that night and offered a simple prayer: "Lord Jesus, I give these dreams back to you. I ask that you protect me where I need protection, wash me where I need washing, lead me where I need leading. I say 'Yes, Lord' and ask that all your desires for me be fulfilled." Now I was finally able to rest in him with some peace.

Searching for Understanding

The search for Christian understanding drove me to read every book, listen to every cassette series, and attend every seminar I could find about dreams. At that time, it meant I read two books, listened to one cassette series, and attended one seminar all by the same author! There was very little Christian material available on dreams which is a sad state for a subject that plays a significant role in the Bible.

Discerning Dreams

However, I found even this small beginning in searching for resources had fruit, for slowly I began to understand that there are different kinds of dreams which helped ease the frustration. Understanding came that not every dream had a deep meaning from God. I could relax, sifting and sorting through dreams, identifying those that might contain a message. If a dream was vague, it was not recorded; if one was long

> **Slowly I was learning to distinguish between natural-process dreams and message dreams.**

and difficult to follow, I let it go. Slowly, I was learning to distinguish between the categories and types of dreams (see chapter 7). This was a very important point, especially in reducing my frustrations. The Holy Spirit was honing my discernment to help me understand which dreams to give time and energy to as dreams from God.

Some of the dreams came with clarity and made my spirit leap with joy. However, some dreams left me with a disturbed spirit, like a dream I had which was full of gangsters chasing me to kill me. I woke in a sweat and great distress, and I knew I could not deal with this dream alone. I needed help.

The Lord places us in the body of Christ, the Church, to help each other, and so, in this case, I shared my dreams with Steve and other close friends and was able to hear what the Lord was saying. The dream of the gangsters spoke of fears I was running from. As we prayed into these dreams, the Lord showed me the fears and healing came.

The point I want to make is that many times the understanding of dreams has evaded me until I have called on Steve or a trusted friend to help me walk through them. This is where Steve and I work together. If you are single or your spouse is not interested in dreams, find a friend whom you trust to help you. We work through the symbols of our dreams within the context of our lives or pray with each other if the dream indicates a need for a deeper listening prayer approach as we have started to use in our counseling sessions. The key we learned was that the Lord wants the Church to function as his body, and as we include his people in our lives, he opens the eyes of our hearts to understand what he is saying.

Over the years, I have grown in my esteem for dreams and in the practical aspects of the dreams in my life. I am certain there is much more to learn. However, the preceding is offered as an encouragement when facing the pitfalls of frustration and discouragement as well as a push into a new excitement toward dreams as a means of personal and corporate communication with our sovereign Creator God.

Conclusion

Ask, and it will be given to you; seek, and you will find; knock, and it will be opened to you. For everyone who asks receives, and he who seeks finds, and to him who knocks it will be opened (Matt 7:7–8).

When we have learned to identify those dreams that contain a message from God, they become a precious communication gift and worth the effort of pressing forward for better understanding. Our Father is interested in a closer relationship with us individually and with the Church as a corporate body. He uses dreams to teach us to seek him, to know him, and to bring us closer to him—the Giver of the dreams.

Chapter Six

Problems Dreaming?

For Those Who Do Not Dream

We would be remiss not to address some of the problems involving the process of dreaming before we enter into the understanding and interpretation process. In every seminar we have conducted, there have been people who claim not to dream, and such people may feel excluded from what God is doing in dreams. Some research has suggested all people dream (see chapter 2). On that basis, it may be more a matter of not remembering dreams than of not dreaming at all. Therefore, we use the following approach with those claiming not to dream as with those not remembering their dreams. Ultimately, it is message dreams from God we would like to receive, and those come at his discretion, not ours. The following suggestions serve only to ensure there is nothing on our part that prevents us from receiving dreams from him when, and if, he chooses to speak to us in that way.

Reasons for Not Remembering Dreams

Here are some reasons you might not remember dreams.

- **Attitude.** If dreams have not been important to you, you will make no effort to remember them. Your attitude toward dreams may determine much about your dream life. Unfortunately, this attitude has often been shaped in children by adults who dismiss them as "only dreams" and therefore of no real importance.

- **Interferences.** An example of interference is the alarm clock or telephone. The shock of these and other disturbances can cause dreams to vanish. Ask God to wake you immediately after receiving a message dream, and be diligent to write it out before going back to sleep.

- **Late nights.** Not enough sleep or over-tiredness can affect dreams and the ability to wake up to record them.

- **Taking medication, drugs, or alcohol.** This needs no further explanation in regard to message dream; however, these things can have negative affects on "natural-process dreams" due to their effect on body chemistry.

- **Pregnancy and menstrual cycles.** The hormone and chemical changes in your body during these times can affect dreams and your memory of dreams.

- **Unwillingness to hear a message from a dream.** There may have been times you were afraid or reluctant to receive the message of a dream.

- **Generational issues.** If, in past generations, an ancestor did anything to dismiss or denounce dreams for any reason, it is possible that act can remain in effect down the lines to the present time.[24] This is easily corrected as explained in the following section.

- **Blocking spirits.** Satan's biggest ploy against God is to damage our ability to enter into and sustain relationship. There are spirits whose role seems to involve continued disruption of relationships. These spirits may hamper dream communication and our relationship with God and others. Blocking spirits are also easily dealt with as we shall explain.

If you think your dreaming is hampered in any way, go through the following points. These may help remove whatever prevents you from receiving or remembering your dreams.

Toward Remembering Dreams

If you are having problems remembering dreams, we recommend the following actions:

- Ensure there is nothing in your attitude preventing you from hearing God. In prayer, confess any poor attitudes toward dreams, ask God's forgiveness, and acknowledge them as important because they are from him.

- Some no longer remember dreams because they have, in the past, ignored the dream message. Confess this, ask forgiveness for ignoring dream messages in the past, and express your desire to learn and to receive dreams from God again, this time with a renewed heart to honor the dream and its message.

- If past generations hold the reason for not remembering dreams, ask forgiveness for anyone in your past generations[25] who may have stopped the communication

knowingly or unknowingly, consciously or uncon-
sciously. Building on that forgiveness, ask God to restart
this means of communication with him.

- To deal with any "blocking spirits," simply ask forgiveness for anything you or those in past generations may
have done to give place to these blocking spirits, then
take authority over them in the name of Jesus, and command them to leave. Ask the Father to fill you with his
Holy Spirit and to speak to you through dreams. It is
very important to remove their "right" to intrude before
commanding them to leave.[26] We recommend you ask
someone to join you in praying through this issue.

- Be prepared to do honor to the communication that
does come to you by being ready to write/record any
dream you receive. The spirit may be willing but the
flesh is weak.[27]

- Wait on the Lord. Dreams may not come every night or
even every week, but prepare yourself for the time you
do receive.

Dream Frequency

How often should we expect to receive message
dreams? That question is impossible to answer in that we
are all different with unique lifestyles, environments, and
at different stages in our relationship with the Father.
Instead of pondering the question, we would do well to
remember that God speaks to us in ways other than
dreams, and placing too much reliance on one method of
communication would deprive us of the benefits of the
others. At times we have received message dreams for several nights as well as several dreams per night. At other

times we experienced weeks without a message dream—we then ask the Father if we are in any way responsible for the absence. We review the suggestions of this chapter to ensure we are not the cause of the void and, if nothing is immediately evident, we set aside our concern, trusting God will speak to us in a dream when it is important.

Conclusion

Do all people dream? Joel 2:28 tells us God will pour his Spirit on all flesh and this will cause us to prophesy, see visions, and dream dreams. The instructions just listed ensure there is nothing on our part that prevents communication through dreams. If you have a close friend from whom you have not heard for awhile, you call them and ask, "Have I done anything to keep you from contacting me?" That question comes out of the desire to be in relationship with the friend. Let it be so in our relationship with the Lord as well. Ask that question of him.

If and/or when dreams start to come, you will want to know how to understand them. In the following chapters, we divide dreams into categories, types, and purposes. These divisions make the work of interpretation easier to conquer by helping to simplify and focus.

Part II

Interpreting...

Then Joseph said to them, "Do not interpretations belong to God?"

Genesis 40:8

And the disciples came and said to Him, "Why do You speak to them in parables?"

Matthew 13:10

Chapter Seven

Types and Purposes of Dreams

reams can seem complex and confusing although usually they are not. To help simplify them, we have divided them into two categories: *miscellaneous dreams* and *message dreams*.

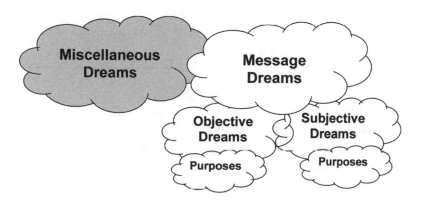

Our focus will be on message dreams, however, we will give a few details regarding miscellaneous dreams as well. To help understand message dreams, we have divided them into two types: *objective* and *subjective* dreams. Both can be given for certain purposes.

Miscellaneous Dreams

One of the first skills we need to learn is to distinguish miscellaneous dreams from message dreams and then to ignore them. That skill comes from knowing there is a difference and by evaluating each dream as it comes. In other words, we learn to differentiate by experience. The majority of our miscellaneous dreams are what we call "natural-process dreams."

Natural-Process Dreams

Many of the dreams we dream will be natural-process dreams, also referred to as "random neuron firings" in the brain. Everyone has these dreams, and, in fact, research has concluded that preventing people from having these dreams for more than a few days will cause them to begin to show signs of mental breakdown. If that is the case (and we have no reason to disagree), we all must dream, and those dreams we call natural-process dreams. We do not believe these dreams carry any particular message. We like to think of them as mental "defrag"[28] to borrow a computer term. Although they have a function in our health and mental well-being, they usually lack the clarity and direction we look for in message dreams. Attempting to understand these natural-process dreams as significant in our lives can lead to the frustration described in chapter 5, "Practical Dreaming," and to the eventual disregard of all dreams.

Body/Chemical Dreams

The body is a mixture of many chemicals. When the body experiences illness or fever, dreams seem to reflect the conflict within. Legal drugs, illegal drugs, or alcohol can also affect dreams, even to the point of becoming nightmares as the body withdraws from the drug.

Pregnancy is a time when the chemicals and hormones of the body are doing strange and wondrous things. This can affect dreams.

Seductive Dreams

This dream type does not fit well under the heading of "miscellaneous dreams" but is experienced by many. We have included it in response to those who have had this experience. Not to be confused with what we often call nightmares, these dreams are under the influence of the demonic—referred to as *incubus* and *succubus* spirits. Because this is a sensitive area with potential for embarrassment, people usually do not talk openly about this type of dream. The following information will help you in understanding the source.

Incubus and *succubus* spirits in dreams are defined as follows: *incubus* (noun; pl. *incubi*) a male demon believed to have sexual intercourse with sleeping women;[29] *succubus* (noun; pl. *succubi*) a female demon believed to have sexual intercourse with sleeping men.[30]

> Incubus: demon in male form that seeks to have sexual intercourse with sleeping women; the corresponding spirit in female form is called a succubus. In medieval Europe, union with an incubus was supposed by some to result in the birth of witches, demons, and deformed human offspring. The legendary magician Merlin was said to have been fathered by an incubus. Parallels exist in many cul-

tures. The word incubus is derived from the Latin *incubus* ("nightmare") and *incubare* ("to lie upon, weigh upon, brood"). In modern psychological usage, the term has been applied to the type of nightmare that gives one the feeling of a heavy weight or oppression on the chest and stomach.[31]

Admittedly, these definitions come from secular sources and need to be filtered through the teaching of Scripture regarding the demonic. However, they do make the point clear. People have been violated in this way, not knowing the source of these dream-like experiences. Until I (Steve) learned of these spirits, I thought the experience was just a natural process dream I had to endure, and these dreams occurred many times over the years. After coming to an understanding of their source, I had a reoccurrence of this type of dream and commanded the spirit to leave in the name of Jesus. The dream ended immediately. If, using this approach, the dream does not end immediately—as it must if it is demonic—treat the dream as any other with symbolism that needs to be understood. If you are still troubled by the dream, look for a counselor with experience in these things who can clarify and resolve this with you.

False Dreams

A person can misuse a dream knowingly or unknowingly for self-serving purposes. Scripture warns us about this.

"Behold, I am against those who have prophesied false dreams [chalom]," declares the LORD, "and related them, and led My people astray by their falsehoods and reckless boasting; yet I did not send

*them or command them, nor do they furnish this
people the slightest benefit," declares the LORD
(Jer 23:32).*

*For the idols have spoken vanity, and the diviners
have seen a lie, and have told false dreams* [chalom]*;
they comfort in vain: therefore they went their way
as a flock, they were troubled, because there was no
shepherd* (Zec 10:2, KJV).

We should evaluate all dreams against the truths of
Scripture. Respond cautiously to the message of any dream.
God can confirm a message in a variety of ways, dreams
being only one.

Message Dreams

When we mention dreams it can be understood that we
are referring to message dreams which are the focus of our
attention in this book. Message dreams usually have a clarity and a sense of purpose to them. These are the dreams the
Father gives to communicate with us. To help understand
our dreams, we divide them into two distinct types and a
combined type by determining who the dream is for.

Subjective and Objective Dreams

To properly understand and respond to our message
dreams, it is imperative to know if the dream is for the
dreamer (subjective) or for someone else (objective). The
concept of using the activity of the dreamer in the dream as
the determining factor for subjective/objective dream types
has strong support when tested against the dreams in the
Bible. Of the twenty dreams and visions listed below, one
does not adhere to this approach as shown.

- Gn 15:1–21—God's covenant with Abraham;
  subjective; correct
- Gn 20:1–18—Abimelech in discussion with God;
  subjective; correct
- Gn 28:10–22—God speaks to Jacob;
  subjective; correct
- Gn 31:10–29—Jacob and God in interaction;
  subjective; correct
- Gn 37:1–11—Joseph's dreams;
  combination; correct
- Gn 40:1–23—Cupbearer and baker;
  subjective; correct
- Gn 41:1–49—Pharaoh's dream of the sevens;
  objective; correct
- Gn 46:1–7—Israel in dialogue with God;
  subjective; correct
- Jgs 7:9–18—Barley loaf hitting the tent;
  objective; correct
- 1 Kgs 3:5–28—God and Solomon interact;
  subjective; correct
- Dn 2:1–49—Statue hit by stone;
  objective; correct
- Dn 4:4–37—Tree cut down;
  subjective; incorrect
- Dn 7:1–28—Four beast coming from the sea;
  objective; correct
- Dn 8:1–27—Ram and goat;
  objective; correct
- Dn 10:1– 12:13—Terrifying vision;
  objective; correct
- Mt 1:20–25—God spoke to Joseph;
  subjective; correct

- Mt 2:3–15—God spoke to Joseph;
  subjective; correct
- Mt 2:19–23—God spoke to Joseph;
  subjective; correct
- Acts 10:9–16—Peter's unclean animals;
  subjective; correct
- Acts 16:9—Paul's Macedonian man;
  subjective; correct

This still equates to 95 percent accuracy which is very good. We have used this method for many years and appreciate its simplicity in differentiating between the subjective and objective dreams.[32]

Subjective Dreams

A subjective dream is given to the dreamer for the dreamer and about the dreamer. Unless you have a calling to the office of prophet[33] or have the gift of prophecy, most (90–95 percent) of your dreams are of this type. The main characteristic of this type of dream is that you play an active part in it.[34] Examples of this type of dream include those of the Pharaoh's baker and cupbearer.[35] In each of their dreams, they played an active role in the dream.

Objective Dreams

An objective dream is given to the dreamer but is not exclusively for the dreamer. The objective dream is one in which the dreamer stands as an observer and does not participate in the activities but watches the events unfold.[36] Examples of this include Daniel's dream of the four beast coming out of the sea[37] and Pharaoh's dream of the cows and the corn.[38] In each of these examples, the dreamer was an observer only. Those called to prophetic offices or gifted in prophecy may experience more of this type of dream.

> *He said, "Hear now My words: If there is a prophet among you, I, the LORD, shall make Myself known to him in a vision [marah]. I shall speak with him in a dream [chalom] (Nm 12:6).*

> *And He gave some as apostles, and some as prophets, and some as evangelists, and some as pastors and teachers, for the equipping of the saints for the work of service, to the building up of the body of Christ (Eph 4:11–12).*

What does one do when given this type of dream? Some big responsibilities go with the objective dream. Of Daniel, we read that he kept the dream to himself.[39] Later, regarding another dream, he was told to keep it a secret.[40] The apostle John was told to write his vision in a book and send it to the seven churches in Asia Minor,[41] and, with no photocopier, making seven copies was no small task. God will make clear to you what you are to do with a dream that pertains to some other person or to the Church. Seek the counsel of one in authority over you before acting, even when there appears to be a clear directive from God. If there is no clear directive, do nothing except to pray into the dream. God shared with Abraham his intentions for Sodom and Gomorrah.[42] Abraham took on the role of intercessor on behalf of those affected—his nephew Lot and family. Whether by directive or intercession, act with discretion, in humility, and in love.

Not all dreams of those called to be prophets will be of the objective type. Rather, many or most of their dreams will be subjective. As we learn to understand our dreams, as we grow proficient in our dream language, and as we show ourselves faithful in the little things,[43] this may change.

Combination Dreams

There may be an occasional dream wherein you have a distinct combination of activity and observation scenes. These dreams may be indicative of an objective dream whose sphere of influence includes you to some degree. Joseph's dream of his brother's sheaves bowing to his is an example of this. In the early part of the dream, he says, *"we were binding sheaves in the field"*[44] which connotes a brief period of activity on Joseph's part, but, in the remainder and larger portion of the dream, his role was an observer. The message of the dream was about his brothers, but it also affected him.

Purposes of Dreams

All message dreams, whether subjective or objective, have purpose and are profitable for our use. Paul tells us the Bible is "inspired" of God, or "God-breathed" (*theopneustos*)—the literal meaning of the Greek word used by the apostle in the following verse:

> *All Scripture is inspired by God and profitable for teaching, for reproof, for correction, for training in righteousness* (2 Tim. 3:16).

The root words of *theopneustos* are the noun *theos* meaning "God" and the verb *pneo* meaning "to blow." This last word is also the root for the word *pneuma* which means "wind" or "breath" but is usually translated "spirit." It gives us a picture of the breath of God or the Spirit of God coming onto the writers of the original text, guiding them into the truth he wanted to be recorded for our benefit.

In the interpretation of dreams, a key principle is that the understanding and interpretation must be in agreement with the teaching and intent of Scripture.

The verse from 2 Timothy tells us that these God-breathed Scriptures are profitable for teaching, reproof, correction, and training. How much of the interaction between a parent and child is covered under these same themes? Our experiences with dreams have found these to be foundational to their function. We would add that dreams are also given to encourage and as an expression of God's love to us.

> In the interpretation of dreams, a key principle is that the understanding and interpretation must be in agreement with the teaching and intent of Scripture.

In the interpretation of dreams, a key principle is that the understanding and interpretation must be in agreement with the teaching and intent of Scripture. For example, the correct interpretation of a dream would never suggest you harm, defraud, or slander a person. These actions are contrary to the command to love one another as we love ourselves. The interpretation of any dream should never contradict God's Word.

We have listed a number of purposes below that apply to either subjective or objective dreams. No doubt this list is not exhaustive, but it may help in understanding the dreams we have.

Vocation dreams

God has a plan for our lives much the same as his statement toward the nation of Israel in Jeremiah 29:11.

'For I know the plans that I have for you,' declares the LORD, *'plans for welfare and not for calamity to give you a future and a hope.*

He will instruct us in the vocation or call he has for our lives as we follow him. This may also include an understanding of our gifts and anointing. In essence, he tells us his plan and purpose for our lives in a vocation dream. This is often done one step at a time.

Dream: I am in the water swimming. It is a large body of water. I am in shallow water. The water is clear and blue. There are huge fish, like the size salmon used to be. The huge fish are all around, going slowly in the general direction of the deeper water. There are lots and lots of them. It is great.

The context was that this dreamer spent a few years on the Canadian west coast where big salmon swim and are a favored meal. From that background, the dreamer understood how big salmon can become and how deep water can be. The dream spoke of water, which, to the dreamer, represented ministry, and the water was very deep. In the dream, the person was swimming in shallow water; even there, however, the person was swimming with the "big fish" representing those already in significant ministry. The direction of the fish indicated a general move into deeper water, representing a move into a deeper level of ministry.

The following are two dreams that I (Steve) had a month apart.

Dream: I was in a house and the owner was there—on my left side. Someone came to the door and dropped off a grey and white mouse. There was another similar but smaller mouse upstairs. The larger mouse went up the stairs to meet the smaller mouse. When it got to the top of the stairs, they met and fought. I ran up to stop them and pulled

them apart. Both were hurt. I carefully cupped my hands under the smaller mouse and carried it downstairs. I showed it to the owner and then, to keep them apart, I placed it in one section of an old cement laundry tub. It did not want to be there and struggled to get out. Finally, it managed to jump up to and crawl over the center divider. As it crawled over, it fell into a pail on that side. The pail was filled with paint cleaner and was white from a previous cleaning. It went under the surface of the cleaner. When it came up, it was all white. It folded its front legs on the top of the pail, rested its chin on its legs, and stayed in that position with a silly contented smile and peaceful look on its face.

Dream: I was in a pond of water. Someone was there—at my left side. While there, a small sparrow fell into the water in front of me. It was in a panic, flapping its wings. It

quickly tired and began to sink. I reached out, cupped my hands under it, and raised it out of the water. I turned to show it to the one beside me and then turned to place it on the ground at the edge of the pool. There, where it would be safe, it could recover and fly again.

On waking from the second dream, I was struck by the similarities to the first dream and asked the Father what they meant. He said, "I want you to help people." At the time, I was already in training as a pastoral counselor, specifically in the prayer counseling ministry that deals with the inner healing of emotions and memories. The "someone" at my side I knew was Jesus, the Wonderful Counselor.[45]

An important point to remember about any "call" to a new vocation is that there is a time for training. Too often we are tempted, after receiving a "call," to run out and begin the work. The calling is not the commissioning, so wait for the commissioning before you act. The Apostle Paul spent three years in Arabia,[46] three years in the *"regions of Syria and Cilicia,"*[47] and one year in Antioch with Barnabas[48] before he was commissioned to do the work of his calling by the Holy Spirit.[49] It was many years after his anointing before David became king of Israel. Do you remember Moses' forty years of training as a leader of large flocks before his commissioning at the burning bush? Our goal must be to follow the Lord, not to run ahead of him.

Cleansing Dreams

Have you ever been around a skunk? The foul odor of the skunk will saturate and penetrate any piece of clothing you wear as well as any exposed part of the body. In short, everything that is near the stench of a skunk will pick up that stench.

We live in an imperfect world, full of spiritual stench, and we are susceptible to picking up "spiritual stuff" just by being out in our normal day. This can occur unknowingly, while walking through a market place, being in the workplace or traveling and so on. Images, sounds, smells, and so on, may have an effect on us and need to be cleansed from our minds and bodies. Cleansing dreams are a way of removing from us the effects of the day. Also, after a time of prayer counseling ministry, it is normal and recommended that counselors pray a cleansing prayer to remove any thoughts or images that may linger and give an opening to the demonic.

My friend and I (Dianne) have had many giggles because of dreams we have had about bathrooms and toilets. At first, there was an embarrassment in sharing dreams of this nature, but we came to learn that these were good dreams to have because they meant we had been cleansed of  something during the night. We did not even have to know what that something was because God was at work, and it was enough for us to just sit back and smile at his care in our lives.

Dream: I was sitting on the toilet going to the bathroom. I felt water dripping on my head. Then I felt water gushing in at me through the mail slot in the door and knew that Steve was clowning around by doing this. I left the toilet, toweling off my wet hair.

When I woke from the dream, I felt washed and cleansed in my spirit by Jesus who was represented by Steve. Again, dreams that involve not only toilets, but also showers, bathrooms, and so on may seem to be an embarrassment to the dreamer, however, we believe they are often good images, representing a cleansing or washing that the Father is doing.

Warning Dreams

Warning dreams exhort us not to do certain things and they sometimes tell us the consequences if we continue. Genesis 20:3 tells us:

But God came to Abimelech in a dream [chalom] *of the night, and said to him, "Behold, you are a dead man because of the woman whom you have taken, for she is married."*

If Abimelech chose to ignore the dream, the consequences would be very serious; he would die!

In Genesis 31:24, God warned Laban not to talk against Jacob:

God came to Laban the Aramean in a dream [chalom] *of the night and said to him, "Be careful that you do not speak to Jacob either good or bad."*

Jacob and his household had fled in secret from Laban; he was afraid of what might happen to him and his wives, children, and livestock when Laban finally caught up with him.

God told Laban, the Syrian, not to speak bad words (threatening, demeaning) to Jacob. However, he was also warning Laban not to speak good words—sweet talk —trying to persuade Jacob to stay with him longer. Laban had tricked Jacob into staying in the past as payment for marriage to his daughters. God's purpose required Jacob to return to the Promised Land as directed in another dream.[50] Laban was not to interfere with those plans.

When he did meet up with Jacob, Laban obeyed what God told him in the dream. Jacob and the well-being of the nation were preserved because of that warning dream.

In Matthew 2:12, God gave a warning dream to the magi:

And having been warned by God in a dream [onar] *not to return to Herod, the magi left for their own country by another way.*

They obeyed the warning and Herod did not have immediate access to God's very own son.

We were approached by a woman with an interest in understanding a dream she had had recently, so she described the dream to us. We listened to her while, at the same time, listening to whatever the Lord might want to say to us about the dream. When she finished, I asked her if she found herself drawn to alcohol or if there was an alcohol problem in her family line. She became very quiet and did not need to hear any more details. She understood the Lord to be warning her about that exact area of her life.

Encouragement Dreams

Sometimes God uses dreams to show us where we are and to encourage us. These dreams motivate us to continue with the things of God.

Dream: There was a buffet. Most people had already gone through the line. I was one of the last people. The bowls were almost empty. There was very little left. I did not really mind because there would be enough. There were two people behind me commenting on the dismal

supply of food. I saw one casserole dish with a lid on it. I touched the lid. It was quite warm. I managed to put the lid to the side and saw the dish held some delicious-looking seafood like shrimp. They were in a cream sauce and I knew I would really like it.

The context was that there was a time when I (Dianne) was struggling with my place of employment. I was feeling like I was in a dry place (not much food left). It was certainly not a "banquet feast" phase in my life. The dream helped me understand that God knew there was some contentment with my work situation (a little food left) and that I was not grumbling or complaining like the other two still going through the line. In the midst of this, the dream provided some encouragement and hope to go on, for though there seemed to be little left, there was still some in a dish. It was being kept warm and it was prepared just the way I, the dreamer, liked it.

Guidance Dreams

Guidance dreams are those that give guidance or direction into the life of the dreamer.

> A vision [horama] *appeared to Paul in the night: a man of Macedonia was standing and appealing to him, and saying, "Come over to Macedonia and help us." When he had seen the vision* [horama], *immediately we sought to go into Macedonia, concluding that God had called us to preach the gospel to them* (Acts 16:9–10).

God spoke to Paul through this vision about a change in plans or a change in direction and Paul responded immediately by arranging a missionary venture into Macedonia.

The Lord knows how we struggle wanting to follow him without knowing where to go. Dreams can be a source of guidance.

In Matthew 2:13–14, we read about a directional dream:

Now when they had departed, behold, an angel of the Lord appeared to Joseph in a dream [onar], saying, "Arise and take the Child and His mother, and flee to Egypt, and remain there until I tell you; for Herod is going to search for the Child to destroy Him." And he arose and took the Child and His mother by night, and departed for Egypt.

God told Joseph to take Mary and Jesus to Egypt and, because Joseph obeyed, the life of God's own son was spared. The dream also told Joseph to remain in Egypt until God gave him further direction.

A pastor's wife accompanied her husband on an interview to a church in the western part of the country. When she saw the parsonage, she recognized the house. She had seen that same house in a dream. The Lord knew she had moved many times in her life and that moving was very hard for her. In his grace and mercy, he prepared her for yet another move by letting her know the next house, inside and out, even before she moved into it. He also assured her that he was directing this change. This also gave confirmation to her husband that the Lord was direct-ing his ministry, this being his next place of service.

I (Steve) had a series of dreams that related to houses. They came weeks apart but they had a common theme.

1) We bought a new house. We were moving in. We had a small black puppy. It was on a leash. When we tried to take it into the new house it struggled against the leash. It did not want to go in but I pulled hard and it went in. The house was very small. Our things would hardly fit into it. We realized this house was too small so we moved back to our old house. This time, the puppy readily jumped into the house. However, when we entered the old house, we found it was also too small.

2) I was shown a house opening or unfolding in different layers into a large house. It was like a 3-D greeting card as it opened.

3) I had a house. It was on a large property. I expanded the house to fill the property.

4) I was working on a project. It involved a round metal bar that reminded me of a similar one I was actually working on, but this one was very big. This project was too big to fit under the roof of the house. As I was watching, the sides and front of our porch expanded by themselves and a new roof formed over the new porch. Now the house was big enough for the job.

Houses in dreams—in my dreams, at least—refer to my personal life. I want you to see the progression of this series of guidance dreams. It starts with the recognition that things were too small and there was resistance to change that needed to be overcome. That change did not bring improvement, and going back was not the solution, showing my thinking had been too small. The second dream showed the unfolding of a new house. The third dream showed the house expanding to fill the property.

The fourth dream showed the ability of the house to grow to meet whatever the need was. I could have missed that series if I had not recorded and reviewed each dream. God had spoken encouragement as he prepared me for a change of direction for my life, and that change has been happening.

Revealing Dreams

The Lord gives dreams that reveal something not known or a future event. Sometimes these revelatory dreams are for the person themselves (subjective) and sometimes they speak of one's family, church, city, or the world (objective). Here is an example of such a dream I (Steve) had and how it helped me:

Dream: I was in my house. A large grizzly bear was trying to get in. It was breaking down the door. I ran to another room and locked the door. The bear started to break that door down. I learned that burning Burl Oak Oil was a bear repellent, so I lit some, expecting the smoke to repel the bear. However, the bear became even more enraged.

The next day, I went to work and purposefully checked one of my projects. This project involved the use of a cutting lubricant that we called "Oak Oil." I found and corrected a small dimensional detail I had missed earlier because it was hidden under a safety guard. That error could have caused someone to be particularly angry. The dream revealed information I needed to know.

Warfare Dreams

Some warfare dreams come from the Lord to expose the plans of our spiritual enemy. Here is an example.

Dream: I saw a black circle with a design in the center that was also black. The whole thing was out of focus. As I watched, it started to come into focus and I saw it was superimposed onto our apartment. As it became clear, I knew it was a satanic symbol coming toward me.

I (Dianne) immediately prayed, even though I did not have any specific understanding of either the dream or the symbol. At breakfast, Steve and I continued to pray against the schemes of the enemy. We persisted by praying at times through the day until we felt peaceful about it. We believe some plan of the enemy for our lives was revealed to us. Knowing in advance allowed us to pray and prevent whatever the enemy had planned.

Warfare dreams can involve the dreamer or others. These dreams may show imagery such as an enemy trying to take our life, shooting at us, stalking us, trying to hurt us, or threatening our lives. There can also be feelings of great fear. These dreams may confirm the hatred of the enemy toward us. We often wrongly label them as "nightmares," but they should be given attention. As children of God, we have a very real enemy who hates God but can do nothing to him. Therefore, he targets the children of God. God, in these dreams, shows us the strategies of the enemy so we can prepare and defeat him.

The following is a dream that I (Steve) had of a battleship.

Dream: I was leading an expedition in a foreign land. We had tents and a small campfire set up beside a stream. I received a note from a messenger. I opened it. The handwritten note read, "I have dispatched a ship to give you protection from the bears." It was signed, "Love, the King." I looked behind me and saw a huge battleship arrayed with impressive guns. As I looked, I understood how it could protect us from land bears but I wondered about polar bears. They could swim  underwater and come up right beside our camp and quickly be in our midst. As this thought passed through my mind I saw the scenario begin to play out. A polar bear entered our camp. I saw a gunner aim a huge cannon and fire. The bear exploded.

I woke from that dream with such excitement Dianne woke up as well. I was excited about the battleship but even more so about the way the note was signed. When I read those words, nothing else mattered. We have often recalled that dream when we felt the "bears" approaching for warfare.

Creativity Dreams

Many people receive creative inspiration through dreams. Our God has given some people new ideas for inventions, and musicians often receive lyrics or tunes that swirl in their minds in the night. In the morning, the dreams yield great fruit. Scientists have been known to receive dreams with important information that led to cures.

Albert Einstein attributed his theory of relativity to a dream from his youth.

> General George Patton received intuitive military guidance from dreams.... Niels Bohr received a Nobel Prize for his quantum theory, which he claimed came from a dream.... Elias Howe had a nightmare that gave him an idea by which he invented the sewing machine.[51]

Here are more examples of those who attribute successes to their dreams:

> The English poet Samuel Taylor Coleridge reported that he had written "Kubla Khan" as the result of creative thinking in a dream. Having fallen asleep while reading about that Mongol conqueror, he woke to write down a fully developed poem he seemed to have composed while dreaming. Novelist Robert Louis Stevenson said that much of his writing was developed by "little people" in his dreams, and specifically cited the story of Dr. Jekyll and Mr. Hyde in this context. The German chemist F.A. Kekulé von Stradonitz attributed his interpretation of the ring structure of the benzene molecule to his dream of a snake with its tail in its mouth. Otto Loewi, the German physiologist, attributed to a dream inspiration for an experiment with a frog's nerve that helped him win the Nobel Prize. In all of these cases the dreamers reported having thought about the same topics over considerable periods while they were awake.[52]

We have a most creative God. Dreams are one way he shares his creative nature with us.

Healing Dreams

This is an exciting and relatively new area within the ministry of inner healing. Used with counseling techniques such as Listening Prayer,[53] Prayer Counseling,[54] TheoPhostic[55] Counseling, and Healing Prayer,[56] dreams are now being used as a key to the deep emotional healing of past memories in the lives of God's people. This inner healing, as it is often called, is an effective tool for bringing change and healing to relationships within the Church. Unfortunately, much of the body is not yet aware of its need or of the existence of this opportunity.

The principle behind inner healing is the person of Jesus. In prayer, we invite Jesus into the memories of our youth. There, he dispels the misunderstandings and lies believed about ourselves by the immature minds of our childhoods. As well, we come face to face with times we have broken one or more of God's spiritual laws during those early years. We are then able to receive forgiveness, cleansing, and restoration through repentance and confession. Jesus has also shown himself to be well able to reach into the generational sins that plague many of us and there break the cycles that affect our lives today.

Jesus is the only one who rightfully owns the title "Wonderful Counselor" (Is 9:6), and he truly is! We have witnessed this fact many times. In the inner healing process, we act as facilitators to his work. This is sometimes easy and sometimes quite demanding. As prayer counselors ourselves, we have seen many people set free from the burdens that damage relationships and experience again the joy of living.

Dreams received by the client, in advance of a counseling appointment, have proven to be invaluable in bringing relief and freedom during the counseling session. We are excited about the new things God is doing with dreams in the healing of memories and have devoted chapter 16 to this topic.

Conclusion

As we learn, through practice, to differentiate between message and miscellaneous dreams and then identify the purpose of the message dream, we are ready for the next step—working with the language of symbols and images. That language deserves to be learned and understood so it can be the precious gift to us it is. When Jesus first spoke to people in parables, the disciples were curious to know what he was saying through those stories. As we will learn in this next chapter, Jesus gave them keys to help get started. Those same principles help us in understanding the language of dreams, as we will see.

Chapter Eight

Approaches to Symbols

W e previously stated that dreams are a sequence of images, symbols, sounds, and emotions with meaning, clarity, and purpose. It is, therefore, important to focus our attention on understanding these images and symbols. There are different approaches to understanding dream symbols/images and we have chosen to present three we think are prominent: the Jungian-Christian, the strict biblical, and the personal-relational approaches. Of these, we will briefly describe the first two of these approaches and devote more time to the last—the one we favor.

Jungian-Christian Approach

This approach, derived from the teaching of Carl Jung and taught at the C.G. Jung Institute in Switzerland, suggests gender in our dreams represents the struggle between the male and female qualities in each of us. Other Christian authors combined this teaching with an interpretation of Genesis 1:27 that reads:

> *God created man in his own image, in the image of God he created him; male and female he created them.*

They suggest this verse teaches we were created with both male and female qualities in each of us. When we dream about other people, we are dreaming about different aspects of our male/female (*anima/animus*) inner selves. It is to an imbalance of this masculine/feminine inner self that our dreams alert us.

We are concerned that this position is an attempt to harmonize things we see in the new sexual norms of society which are actually the result of the fall of humanity and should not be blamed on our creation. When we test the Jungian approach to the dreams of Scripture it does not hold true; therefore, we would be cautious in using it. Look at the following verse as an example:

> *A vision* [horama] *appeared to Paul in the night: a man of Macedonia was standing and appealing to him, and saying, "Come over to Macedonia and help us"* (Acts 16:9).

The Jungian approach would suggest the man calling Paul is his own masculine self. The Jungian analyst may suggest Paul's celibate lifestyle pushed him to reject or subdue his masculine qualities, placing him in an imbalanced state. The dream man was calling to him for acceptance. Because Jung did not begin with the fear of the Lord or the knowledge of the Holy One, he had no plumb line against which to measure any of his theories. We know from Scripture that God was simply calling Paul to evangelize the people in Macedonia.

Strict Biblical Approach

Another approach contends that every symbol in our dreams must *always* match the meaning of the symbol given in Scripture. This suggests that all symbols mean the same thing for every person. Sometimes, and with some symbols, this approach may hold true but never always. For example, water can represent the Holy Spirit in the Bible; however, in dreams, I would never press the point that water in a roadside ditch must also represent the Holy Spirit.

Personal-Relational Approach

Both of the above approaches fall short in respect to the personal relationship we have with our Father through Jesus Christ. We believe the meaning of the symbols and images has to be simple and personal—simple, because in all of God's interactions with us we see the elegance of simplicity. We will show you what we mean. How many regulations did the teachers of the law, in Jesus' day, demand of the people? Read Matthew 23 for a look at some of their rules and of Jesus' opinion of them. Conversely, all of the Law is summarized in these two commandments: to love God above all and to love your neighbor as yourself.[57]

> As a rule, keep the meaning of the symbols simple and personal to the dreamer.

The simplicity of the gospel message is what baffles the wise.

At that time Jesus said, "I praise you, Father, Lord of heaven and earth, because you have hidden these things from the wise and learned, and revealed them to little children" (Mt 11:25, NIV).

I tell you the truth, anyone who will not receive the kingdom of God like a little child will never enter it (Lk 18:17, NIV).

Read again the parables of Jesus and notice the simplicity of each. This applies to dreams, too. As a rule, keep the meaning of the symbols simple.

The meaning of symbols and images should also be kept personal. In a dream, God draws from our minds the symbols and images of our life experiences. These symbols and images he weaves into the message of the dream. Look again at the Genesis 40 dreams of the baker and his bread or the cupbearer squeezing grapes—very personal use of symbols in each case.

Remember Peter's trance in Acts 10:11—

...and he beheld the sky opened up, and a certain object like a great sheet coming down, lowered by four corners to the ground....

The Greek word for sheet is *othone* which means, "fine linen, fine linen cloths, sails, a sail."[58] Notice the word "sail" listed as one of the meanings. Peter was a sailor and fisherman. God used the symbol of a sail to present the unclean animals to Peter. This very personal use of a symbol would grab Peter's attention and perhaps remind him of Jesus' words, "Follow me, and I will teach you to catch men."[59] Interesting, too, is that those words of invitation were not spoken to Matthew, a tax collector, but to Peter and Andrew, both fishermen. As a rule, keep the meaning of the symbols personal to the dreamer.

If you do not have the kind of relationship with Jesus in which you know him as your friend and as your Lord, you are missing a very wonderful experience. Should you want that experience, please read the following prayer, and if it expresses your desire, read it again to him:

> Lord Jesus, I have sinned in the past and expect I will sin in the future.[60] I understand these sins, and my tendency to sin, separate me from relationship with you.[61] I understand you died on the cross, paying the price for the sin[62] of all who believe this, so we can stand before God in your perfection.[63] It is my desire to receive your payment for my past, present, and future sin, so please be the payment for all my sin. Lord, from this moment on, all my sin has been paid for and nothing now separates me from being in relationship with you—I thank you.[64] Lord, please fill me with your Holy Spirit now, too,[65] teaching me the details of what has just happened to me, and especially teach me to grow in my new relationship with you.[66] Thank you, Jesus; I look forward to getting to know you.

Please tell someone that you have made the decision to be in close relationship with Jesus.[67]

Conclusion

As we read the dreams of the Bible, we see the simple and personal approach to understanding those dreams. Out of relationship and over time, God establishes a personal dream vocabulary, a picture dictionary with each person today, as well. This is the subject of the next chapter. "Simple and personal" also implies we can understand our dreams. As we begin to learn our dream vocabulary, communication can be slow and labored, but with persistence and practice comes improvement and fluency.

To identify and understand the symbols, we need to diffuse the frustration we all experience when we approach our dreams. Frustration is probably the major blockage to that understanding. In the next chapter, we will de-mystify the realm of symbols and images by showing you are already familiar with them, and they are very common to our everyday lives.

Chapter Nine

Basic Dream Language

*W*e want to take you on a short journey to show you that symbols and images are a normal part of our daily lives not an abnormality. If we can convince you this language is normal and simple, a good portion of our struggle in understanding dreams will be behind us. Understanding dreams can become as simple as reading:

> **reading** (activity) Activity characterized by the translation of symbols, or letters, into words and sentences that have meaning to the individual.[68]

Reading is the translation of symbols into words and sentences. This sounds very much like dream interpretation. We learned to read by persistence and practice in the task of interpreting the symbols and images into words and sentences which began to have meaning to us. It is fascinating to watch someone learn a new language or to watch a child wrestle with communication. Imagine the frustration of parents trying to understand what their child is saying in the early stages of learning to talk. Do they want something? Are they hurt? How do they want us to help them? What are they saying? Not only are parents frustrated, the child is as well. The communication problem exists until the symbols and images used to represent words and sounds are understood.

One of the first words—other than "mama" and "dada"—many children become proficient with is "cookie." They learn the relationship of the sound of that word to an object that interests them. They learn to associate words like nose, chin, ears, and so on, with objects on their face. Children learn to read by association. Do you remember the flash cards, "A is for Apple," "B is for Ball," "C is for Cat," and the pictures that represented the use of the long and short vowels?

A is for

As we mastered the names of all these pictures and objects, we took the next step. Do you remember your early school readers and how well illustrated they were with large colorful pictures representing the text of a story, i.e. "See Spot Run"? We associated the names of these pictures and

114

objects with words that
represented action: "throw
ball," "ear hurt," and
"tummy hungry." Words
like "sleepy" and "tired"
were some of few that
seemed difficult to master
in those early years.

Next, we add the rest of the fluff, the grammar, to form
sentences. Now we are understood—well, almost. Some
sentences, such as "Read the instructions carefully!" or "Do
you like my new dress?" and a few others may never be
properly understood.

Do you remember the fable of the hare and the tortoise?

What did it teach? What are we to learn from
sayings such as "A bird in the hand is worth
two in the bush,"
or "Don't bite the
hand that feeds
you"?
Have you tried to
learn a second
language? Many methods start by

teaching the names of objects known to us—dog, cat, cow,
father, mother, brother, sister, and so on. To these, we add
the action or descriptive words and then the rest of the
words to make phrases and sentences.

Do all these associations stop as we grow up? Not at all!
You cannot talk or listen for more than a few minutes without encountering a word picture. They are "like copper
pennies"—cheap and plentiful. Telling you this is not "letting the cat out of the bag" and you do not have to "wait

until the cows come home." Everyone "on God's green earth" uses them and, through practice, these mysterious phrases have become as "clear as the nose on your face" to those who use and hear them. These phrases are the word pictures of metaphors, similes, and metonymies.

Metaphors, Similes, and Metonymies

metaphor (mèt´e-fôr´,–fer; noun) A figure of speech in which a word or phrase that ordinarily designates one thing is used to designate another, thus making an implicit comparison.[69] The phrases "walk a mile in his shoes" or "he is just blowing steam" are examples of metaphors.

simile (sîm´e-lê; noun) A figure of speech in which two essentially unlike things are compared, often in a phrase introduced by *like* or *as*.[70] For example "growing like weeds" or "quick as lightning" are similes.

metonymy (me-tòn´e-mê; noun) A figure of speech in which one word or phrase is substituted for another with which it is closely associated.[71] An example of this may be a referral to the Bible as the "sword" or to a car as your "wheels."

Metaphors, similes, and metonymies use a symbol or word picture to represent something else. This is the language used by Jesus throughout the gospels. Here is a wonderful example of a simile:

"O Jerusalem, Jerusalem…! How often I wanted to gather your children together, the way a hen gathers her chicks under her wings, and you were unwilling" (Matt 23:37).

116

Can you picture the beautiful symbolism—a hen with chicks under her wings—that this represents? It is the perfect way of planting a truth into our mind. It is not easily forgotten and was common and personal to the people of that time.

> The dream language is not some weird exception to reality; it is the rule— we grew up with it, we live with it.

The following is a very small sample of the metaphors and similes commonly used in everyday conversation. I am sure, as you give attention to hearing the word pictures, you will smile and be amazed at the frequency and variety prevalent in our culture. They are used so often we do not even notice them. They are very humorous and common in everyday speech:

fly in the ointment

straight as an arrow

I could eat a horse

money down the drain

he's all thumbs

snug as a bug in a rug

I'm in over my head

keep your shirt on

till the cows come home

once in a blue moon

lock, stock, and barrel

ugly as a mud fence

all the tea in China

a broken record

flogging a dead horse

flat as a pancake

miles apart

chomping at the bit

wrench in the works

water off a duck's back

can't see the forest for the trees

the squeaky wheel gets the oil

nothing to sneeze at

so tight he squeaks

he's worth his weight in salt

hold your horses

playing with fire

happy as a pig in slop

packed like sardines

a feather in your cap

smelling like a rose

through the ringer

feel all fenced in

raining cats and dogs

tip of the iceberg

growing like weeds

From all these phrases, can you see how the use of symbols or word pictures is a normal part of our lives?

The dream language is not some weird exception to reality; it is the norm. We grew up with it, we live with it.

Symbolism and the Bible

Every covenant from God had symbolism. We have the rainbow, the cross, the empty tomb, the dove, the bread, the fruit of the vine, the sword, the armor of God, and so on.

Remember the twenty-third psalm with all its images and pictures? The Bible is replete with word pictures; even people's names in the Bible had important meaning. In your dreams, pay attention to the names of people whenever they are given.

The following are only the result of a quick glance through the Bible. Look them up for context if you are interested, or just skim though the list. This is not an exhaustive list. There are many more in Scripture:

- *My* (rain)*bow* (Gn 9:13)
- *count the stars* (Gn 15:5)
- *a smoking oven and a flaming torch* (Gn 15:17)
- *a wild donkey of a man* (Gn 16:12)
- *the dust of the earth* (Gn 28:14)

- *Every place on which the sole of your foot treads* (Jos 1:3)
- *a loaf of barley bread was tumbling into the camp* (Jgs 7:13)
- *Have You not made a hedge about him and his house* (Jb 1:10)
- *like a tree firmly planted by streams* (Ps 1:3)
- *The LORD is my shepherd* (Ps 23:1)
- *Thy rod and Thy staff, they comfort* (Ps 23:4)
- *prepare a table before me* (Ps 23:5)
- *like chaff before the wind* (Ps 35:5)
- *As the deer pants for the water brooks* (Ps 42:1)
- *cover you with His pinions* (Ps 91:4)
- *all is vanity and striving after wind* (Eccl 1:14)
- *Your eyes are like doves* (Songs 1:15)
- *like a gazelle... on the mountains of spices* (Songs 8:14)
- *Though your sins are as scarlet, They will be as white as snow; Though they are red like crimson, They will be like wool* (Is 1:18)
- *broken the staff of the wicked* (Is 14:5)
- *like poplars by streams of water* (Is 44:4)
- *Heaven is My throne and the earth is My footstool* (Is 66:1)
- *fountain of living waters... Broken cisterns* (Jer 2:13)
- *like a choice vessel* (Jer 25:34)
- *like a bear lying in wait, Like a lion* (Lam 3:10)
- *like glowing metal in the midst of the fire* (Ez 1:4)
- *like a vessel in which no one delights* (Hos 8:8)
- *like a lion to them; like a leopard* (Hos 13:7)
- *like an ever-flowing stream* (Am 5:24)
- *like the creeping locust... the swarming locust* (Na 3:15)
- *He has made my feet like hinds' feet* (Hb 3:19)
- *like a refiner's fire and like fullers' soap* (Mal 3:2)
- *skip about like calves from the stall* (Mal 4:2)

- *Look at the birds of the air* (Mt 6:26)
- *Observe how the lilies of the field grow* (Mt 6:28)
- *like the surf of the sea, driven and tossed* (Jas 1:6)
- *the devil, prowls around like a roaring lion* (1 Pt 5:8)
- *the day of the Lord will come like a thief* (2 Pt 3:10)

  And His head and His hair were white like white wool, like snow; and His eyes were like a flame of fire; and His feet were like burnished bronze, when it has been caused to glow in a furnace, and His voice was like the sound of many waters. And in His right hand He held seven stars; and out of His mouth came a sharp two-edged sword; and His face was like the sun shining in its strength (Rv 1:14–16).

  And I heard, as it were, the voice of a great multitude and as the sound of many waters and as the sound of mighty peals of thunder, saying, "Hallelujah! For the Lord our God, the Almighty, reigns" (Rv 19:6).

The Book of the Revelation of Jesus Christ is full of word pictures and most of us have the impression of it being hard to understand with its weird images. This is because the language uses many metaphors and similes. This revelation comes to us from Jesus and carries a blessing, as the first verse states.

  Blessed is he who reads and those who hear the words of the prophecy, and heed the things which are written in it; for the time is near (Rv 1:3).

Try to read it again when you have a firm grasp of the concepts of dream and vision symbols and images. You may be surprised.

The Parables of Jesus

The Gospels abound with symbols in the parables of Jesus. When Jesus started to use parables to teach the people truths about the King-
dom of God, his disciples did not understand the message. They confronted Jesus about the difficulties "the people" were having, but Jesus understood the real question, as we read:

> It is interesting that Jesus speaks to us, in our dreams, using the same kind of language he used in parables— the language of metaphor, simile, and metonymy.

And the disciples came and said to Him, "Why do You speak to them in parables?" And He answered and said to them, "To you it has been granted to know the mysteries of the kingdom of heaven, but to them it has not been granted" (Mt 13:10–11).

What is the definition of a parable?

parable (pàr´e-bel; noun) A simple story illustrating a moral or religious lesson.[72]

Notice that the word "parable" is derived from the words "from," "to compare," "beside" —these are the Greek roots for the word "parable." They refer to using one thing as a comparison to another thing, or of using one thing as a parallel illustration of something else. Parables are not confined to the New Testament.

I have also spoken to the prophets, And I gave numerous visions [chazon]; And through the prophets I gave parables [damah: to be like, resemble] (Hos 12:10).

121

In these first two parables, Jesus gives us the meaning of the symbols and these meanings become the keys that help us understand and develop meanings for the word pictures in the other parables. These keys become the foundation on which we build a picture dictionary helping us to understand the other parables. While telling the rest of his parables, he gradually adds to the symbols and modifies them to vary their meaning in relation to the context of the story.

To help you to develop the skills needed for your own dictionary of dream symbols, we will walk through these first two parables together using tables. You will need to read each parable carefully as you work through the associated table. Be careful, because not all the words in our versions of the Bible are actually in the Greek text; many are added for flow or to complete a sentence, such as the word "seed" in the first parable.

The Sower's Seed: Matthew 13:1–23

Symbol Used	Revealed Meaning
sower	no meaning given
what is sown	word of the kingdom
roadside soil	hear, but lose to birds
rocky soil	hear, but no depth
thorny soil	hear, but are choked
good soil	hear and bear fruit
birds	the evil one
thorns	the cares of this world

Tares: Matthew 13:24–30 and 13:36–43

Symbol Used	Revealed Meaning
sower	Son of Man
field	the world
good seed (wheat)	the sons of the kingdom
enemy	the evil one
bad seed (tares)	the sons of the evil one
slaves	angels
harvest	the end of the age
barn	the kingdom of God

Enjoy this good exercise, because the same principles can be used to develop your personal dream picture dictionary.

Conclusion

The language of dreams is much more natural to us than we are first aware. Our objective was to de-mystify the language and to encourage development of proficiency with symbols and imagery. As in the study of any foreign language, proficiency comes with practice. After that investment, understanding dreams will be almost second nature. Jesus' statement to the disciples regarding his reason for speaking in parables includes these words:

> *To those who are open to my teaching, more understanding will be given, and they will have an*

abundance of knowledge. But to those who are not listening, even what they have will be taken away from them (Mt 13:12, NLT).

There are, or seem to be, some symbols we can consider common or basic. They provide a starting point or foundation on which we build our understanding of the language of dreams.

Chapter Ten

Some Basic Symbols

*D*ream: I was in a boxing ring waiting for the bell to start the first round. I was told to do nothing. The bell sounded. We moved and danced around but did nothing. The bell sounded to end the round. I sat down in my corner. The bell sounded again to start round two so I got up and went in. We jabbed at each other. I hit him, he missed  me. I threw a left/right combo and he went down for the count. I went back to my corner and said, "I got him." My trainer said, "I knew you could do it."

This is worth repeating: we need to be *very careful* with someone else's list of symbols. It could be like reading their love letter and taking it to be our own. We lack the history or context that makes the letter special to the one to whom it was sent. I (Steve) was a boxer for a couple years and the dream means much to me for that reason.

The meaning of symbols can change or be modified even for the same dreamer. For that reason, you should be careful not to make any meaning absolute. Many symbols can represent different things. Consider the picture of the "lion." It can represent Jesus as the "Lion of Judah," Satan as a "roaring lion," or something very different to someone in another country where lions are a danger. There almost seems to be a good and an evil meaning to symbols. Evaluate each meaning using details from the dream such as the color of the symbol, the posture, the eyes, the size, and especially the emotions you felt during the dream. These all hold a key to understanding the symbols.

Give attention to the age of symbols, such as the home of your youth versus your present home. This is important, especially in healing, because it helps to identify the timing of the message. Many symbols can have biblical and a variety of personal meanings. Which meaning do you choose? Searching for God's message in your dream requires you to be very honest with yourself. We might choose to believe one meaning over another because one is more favorable. However, doing so will rob us of the truth and of the benefits of the message. We believe there will be a witness in our spirit when we have the correct meaning and a gnawing feeling if we draw the wrong meaning. This, too, is part of the process of growing into an understanding of our dream language.

The following are symbols that seem to be common to people in our culture. Please be careful with these. We ask you to consider them as stepping stones to building your own understanding of the message.

Buildings

Generally, buildings represent more static or stationary facets of your life.

- House: your personal life
- High rise: your life in community or your church
- Cottage: your spare time, relaxation
- Factory: your job, vocation

Rooms

Rooms are related to buildings and important because they focus more closely on a specific area of your life.

- Bedroom: place of intimacy
- Bathroom: place of cleansing
- Living room: day-to-day living
- Basement: things under the surface
- Closet: hidden areas of your life
- Classroom: place of learning

Vehicles

The activities of your life can be represented by vehicles.

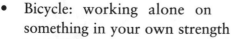

- Bicycle: working alone on something in your own strength
- Motorcycle: working alone on something with power
- Unicycle: alone and precarious
- Car: a ministry or vocation with room for others

127

- Bus: a church/community ministry
- Taxi: someone is taking you for a ride

Airplanes

Airplanes are generally a matter of a higher spiritual position or ministry, the scope of which is depicted by the size of the plane.

- Small: your personal spiritual ministry
- Big: community/church ministry
- Jet: fast-paced
- Glider: coming down—no power

Ships and Boats

These are similar to vehicles but have a more global scale, because they are not limited to traveling on land.

Dream: I was fishing with others. They were in canoes and I was on a flat board. We went to different parts of the world to fish.

Was my outlook too small for God's plans? One year to the day later, we landed in Australia on a teacher exchange made possible by the school board.

Action

As you may expect, action in a dream can be an indication or description of progress and achievement.

- Running: lots of activity
- Hiding: not venturing out

- Climbing: progressing in your own strength
- Walking: slow progress
- Flying: reaching new spiritual heights
- Floating: being supported by the Spirit

People

Contrary to Jungian thought, we believe people in subjective dreams can represent what they are in relationship to us or what their character represents to us. It is also important to pay attention to the roles and names of people in your dreams, especially if the name is spoken. People's names have meaning and may be important to the dream. For example, the name "Anne" means grace. I have often had my sister Anna walking with me in dreams. An older brother may, as in my dreams, represent Jesus.

- Father, or grandfather: God the Father
- Mother: God the Spirit
- Brother: Jesus
- Babies: a new thing coming into your life
- A teacher: the Holy Spirit
- A mystery person next to you: Jesus or the Holy Spirit

Animals

When dreaming of an animal, generally look to the characteristic of the animal. Some are listed below and obviously these are mainly North American animals. Whatever the country, learn the trait of local animals—especially if you do not have personal history with them. These meanings change much with the background or lifestyle of the dreamer.

- Lion: courage; authority; Jesus; Satan
- Bear: rage, anger, demonic attack
- Sheep: Christians; meek
- Snake: demonic involvement
- Spider: demonic presence
- Bees: demonic annoyance
- Fish: evangelistic ministry
- Dogs: faithfulness; human attack

Water

In Scripture, water is often representative of the Holy Spirit, but it is important not to be stuck on this one interpretation. Look at more than the presence of water. Find the source or the quality of the water to get some direction in the understanding of water. By this, I mean fresh, clear, dirty, stagnant, flowing, and so on; these qualities have a significant impact on the meaning. An acquaintance was stuck on the understanding that water in his dream referred to the Holy Spirit, even though the water was dripping out of a garbage bin.

- River: the flow/move of the Spirit
- Ditch: the flow/ways of the world
- Lake: the work of the Kingdom
- Ocean/sea: the world

- Pond: local community
- Current: fast progress
- Rapids: fast with perils

Colors

Colors can have both a biblical and a personal meaning.

- Red: blood atonement; alert; danger
- Orange: courage; praise; warning
- Yellow: glory; fear; warning
- Blue: revelation; heaven; depression
- Purple: royalty; authority; kingship
- Black: evil; sin; death
- White: purity; holiness; righteousness
- Green: everlasting life; new beginning; safety
- Rainbow: covenant

Numbers

The meanings of numbers as listed below usually come from the Bible. For example, the number six comes from the fact that human beings were created on the sixth day. Again, if a particular number has a special meaning to you, give it serious consideration in respect to your dreams.

- 1: beginning; singleness; God
- 2: union; witness
- 3: Godhead; perfect testimony
- 4: earth-related

- 5: grace; ministry
- 6: humankind; humanity
- 7: God; completeness; perfection
- 8: fullness; new beginning; Holy Spirit
- 9: blessing; fruitfulness
- 10: law; trial; testing; human government
- 11: lawlessness; incompleteness
- 12: divine government
- 30: sorrow; maturity
- 40: testing; trial
- 50: celebration; ceremony; jubilee
- 70: judgments and human committees

Conclusion

We hesitated in providing these symbols because we believe strongly in the personal approach to dream symbols. Providing any list creates opportunity to misuse the information. Our list is offered to give you examples of the use of symbols as a guide not a solution to the meaning of your symbols. You will, over time, develop your own personal dictionary of dream symbols with meanings that will likely differ from those in this list. Prayerfully consider the meaning of your symbols or discuss the symbol with someone close to you to come to an understanding of your dream language.

The last issue of importance in understanding the dream, especially subjective dreams, involves context. When you dream, make a note of the context—the events in your life at the time of the dream—because a big part of the equation in the full understanding of your dreams is the matter of context. It is in the context of our lives at the time of the dream that the symbols begin to make sense and lead to understanding.

Chapter Eleven

Context of the Dream

*I*magine a day in the life of a farm family with twelve sons. The youngest son is obviously the father's favorite. This son regularly reports to his father the misdeeds of the brothers. This activity does not earn him their favor.

It is harvest time and the family is out cutting and tying the grain into bundles to dry. The youngest son is working beside his father; rather, he is clowning around and entertaining his father more than working. The others are working hard wanting to please their father, but they do not receive his praise or attention as does their little brother.

That night, the favored son has a dream....

He said to them, "Listen to this dream [chalom] *I had: We were binding sheaves of grain out in the field when suddenly my sheaf rose and stood upright, while your sheaves gathered around mine and bowed down to it." His brothers said to him, "Do you intend to reign over us? Will you actually rule us?" And they hated him all the more because of his dream* [chalom] *and what he had said* (Gn 37:6–8, NIV).

As you have figured out by now, the context we have given is not recorded in the Bible but could well have been close to the actual situation. The personal aspects of the dream symbols are present regardless of the background we have added. This is a good example of a combination dream (subjective/objective); the meaning the message is for others but affects the dreamer. We notice Joseph is active at the beginning of the dream by binding sheaves, but in the later, and larger,

> **The context of the dreamer's life at the time of the dream is often a key to understanding the symbols and the meaning of that dream.**

part of the dream, Joseph is an observer. His second dream about the sun, moon, and eleven stars, however, is objective and meant for the others.

Since context is very important in understanding the message of a dream, interpretation of another person's dream is more difficult, and we should be cautious in attempting to interpret them apart from a clear direction from the Holy Spirit.

The context of the dreamer's life at the time of the dream is often a key to understanding the symbols and the meaning of that dream. It is as important to the dream as color is to a traffic light—green, yellow, or red each give a very different message, yet all are lights. It is dangerous to approach another person's dream without prayer, without an intimate understanding of the circumstances in the life of that person, and/or a divine directive and anointing for the interpretation of dreams.

Dream: I was looking at a koala. It was half buried in the sand and appeared to be dead. My sister was there and pulled it out of the sand by the ear. It suddenly started to squirm so she let go of it and we watched it run to a tree and climb upward.

What could that possibly mean? What personal context does someone from North America have with a koala? Putting the dream into the context of my (Steve) life at the time of the dream holds the key to the meaning. Dianne and I were in the process of applying for a teacher exchange to Australia (koala). Progress seemed to have come to a halt (stuck in the sand) and a deadline was quickly approaching. Our prayers and a phone call (the ear), with the help of the Holy Spirit (sister), released the process (pulled it up), helping to get important paperwork moving again (climbing) in time for the due date. This book was finished while in Australia.

Symbol/Picture	Meaning
koala	exchange to Australia
buried in the sand	progress halted
sister	Holy Spirit
pulled it out	revived
by the ear	prayers and phone calls
climbing	progress continues

Dream: A black dog approached me. It acted "weasel-like." I knew it was trying to get behind me to bite me. I held my attaché case in front of me to block its advance. The dog tried to get under my case.

What did it mean? Let me add the following context information and see if it helps. At the time of the dream, I had a colleague who was berating my work to others behind my back. Can you fill in this table now?

Symbol/Picture	Meaning
black dog	
weasel-like	
behind me	
to bite	
attaché case	

I believe the Father wanted me to be aware of the situation. He is very much interested in our daily lives. I experienced strength and encouragement just realizing he was aware of what I was going through. No directive was given in the dream, so we began to pray for that colleague.

You can see that knowing the context of a dream can be a very important key to knowing its meaning. Context is simply those events active in the life of the dreamer at the time of the dream and, as the example shows, context is very important in bridging the gap between the dream and the interpretation of the dream.

Bridge

As a further illustration of context, what do you think of when you hear the word "bridge"? Do you think of the steel structure that forms an arch over a river, or maybe a pattern of ropes and boards swaying as it spans the sides of a canyon? A banker may think of a type of financial transaction, and a dentist may see one or more replacement teeth held in place by natural teeth. An optometrist pictures the bridge of a nose supporting corrective lenses, while the violinist thinks of the bridge that holds the strings taut and high above the soundboard. The thoughts of a *Star Trek* fan will be transported to the bridge of the USS Enterprise. For others, it could be the bridge of a cruise ship, a card game, a narrow strip of land between two continents, or a rest used to support the pool cue in a difficult shot. To the engineering type, it might be a special type of electrical circuit, the connection between atoms or molecules, or it could be some other entity or concept in a field we have not yet bridged. This is only one example of how important the background of the dreamer is to the context of a dream.

We find there can be a delay of one or more days between an event (the context) and the dream. When you record your dreams, remember to look back a number of days to see if there is some key there and include it with the dream. It is also possible the key will come in the days ahead. If the meaning does not seem evident, set it aside and wait; only do not let frustration cloud your insights (metaphorically speaking, of course).

Daniel gives an interesting picture that tells of a cause for delay he experienced in answer to one of his prayers:

> *Then* (the angel) *said to me, "Do not be afraid, Daniel, for from the first day that you set your heart on understanding this and on humbling yourself before your God, your words were heard, and I have come in response to your words. But the prince of the kingdom of Persia was withstanding me for twenty-one days; then behold, Michael, one of the chief princes, came to help me, for I had been left there with the kings of Persia"* (Dn 10:12–13).

It was important that, from the moment Daniel prayed, God had sent an answer. Even in this discourse between the angel and Daniel, we see symbolism in the phrase "the prince of the kingdom of Persia." This phrase had meaning to Daniel. At the time of the vision, Daniel was under the authority of Cyrus, king of Persia. However, we know no human king or prince could stop an angel with a message from God. For that reason, we have taken this term "the prince of the kingdom of Persia" to be symbolic for a ruler, a power, a world force of darkness, or a spiritual force of wickedness as described in Ephesians 6:12. The term "prince of the kingdom of Persia" may have been as common a term to Daniel in his culture as the term "the forces of darkness" is to us today.

Conclusion

Context is very important in helping us understand the meaning of our dreams. This is especially so in regard to our subjective dreams—those dreams for and about ourselves. Objective dreams, being for others or for the Church, may not be understood in the context of the dreamer's personal life but more so in the context of the life of those for whom the dream's message was intended. This brings many questions to the fore regarding the proper approach or response to dreams we receive.

Chapter Twelve

Responding to Dreams

---

*D*reams require an appropriate response. This becomes evident by examining the way people responded to dreams they received as recorded in the Bible. In particular, the Book of Daniel contains some fascinating stories from the life of King Nebuchadnezzar from which we will learn how to properly respond to dreams.

The King's First Dream

Nebuchadnezzar had dreams [chalom] *and his spirit was troubled and his sleep left him* (Dn 2:1).

The King's Response

Nebuchadnezzar's response to this dream was to gather his *"magicians, the conjurers, the sorcerers and the Chaldeans, to tell the king his dreams"* (v. 2). They informed the king that it was impossible for anyone to tell the king the meaning of his dream. The king's response was fury. He ordered all wise men to be destroyed. After the decree went out, they looked for Daniel and his friends because they were to be killed as well (v. 13).

Daniel's Response

Daniel's first action was to go to the king and ask for time so he might come up with the dream and the interpretation (v. 16). When the king agreed, Daniel's next response was to return to his friends; together they requested:

> ...*compassion from the God of heaven concerning this mystery, so that Daniel and his friends might not be destroyed with the rest of the wise men of Babylon* (v. 18).

Daniel's Vision/Dream

It was in a night vision that the *"mystery was revealed to Daniel"* (v. 19). God gave Daniel the king's dream.

Daniel's Response

Upon receiving the night vision of the king's dream, Daniel's first response was to bless the God of heaven (vv. 19–23). He was granted an audience with the king as the *"man among the exiles from Judah who can make the interpretation known to the king"* (v. 25). When the king asked if he was the one able to do this, Daniel responded by denouncing all the wise men, conjurers, magicians, and diviners as not being able to. He then declared that *"there is a God in heaven who reveals mysteries, and He has made known to the king what will take place in the latter days"* (v. 28). A very important issue now arises. God's purpose in giving Daniel the wisdom for this dream is explained as *"for the purpose of making the interpretation known to the king, and that you may understand the thoughts of your mind"* (v. 30). Daniel tells the king his dream.

> *You, O king, were looking and behold, there was a single great statue; that statue, which was large and of extraordinary splendor, was standing in front of you, and its appearance was awesome. The head of that statue was made of fine gold, its breast and its arms of silver, its belly and its thighs of bronze, its legs of iron, and its feet partly of iron and partly of clay. You continued looking until a stone was cut out without hands, and it struck the statue on its feet of iron and clay and crushed them. Then the iron, the clay, the bronze, the silver and the gold were crushed all at the same time and became like chaff from the summer threshing floors; and the wind carried them away so that not a trace of them was found. But the stone that struck the statue became a great mountain and filled the whole earth* (Dn 2:31–35).

Daniel began to reveal the details of the dream depicting the king as the head of gold and the kingdoms that followed having less splendor, down to the eventual feet made of the poor mixture of clay and iron. Then a stone, cut "not by hands," smashed the statue to powder to be blown away in the wind.

The King's Response to the Dream

The king responded immediately. He fell on his face, offering homage to Daniel and then to God.

> *The king answered Daniel and said, "Surely your*
> *God is a God of gods and a Lord of kings and a*
> *revealer of mysteries, since you have been able to*
> *reveal this mystery"* (Dn 2:47).

Daniel was given many gifts and promoted to ruler over the entire province of Babylon and allowed to dwell in the king's court. All the other wise men were made subject to Daniel while his friends, Shadrach, Meshach, and Abednego, were appointed administrators over the province.

The King's Next Two Responses

However, King Nebuchadnezzar's heart response to God did not last long. He made a golden image of himself and ordered all to bow to it. The Chaldeans saw an opportunity to destroy the three Judeans who were in authority over them. Shadrach, Meshach, and Abednego were thrown into the furnace. Once again, the king witnessed the power of God when Daniel's three friends were saved from the fire, and Nebuchadnezzar responded with the following:

> *"Blessed be the God of Shadrach, Meshach, and*
> *Abednego, who has sent His angel and delivered His*
> *servants who put their trust in Him, violating the*
> *king's command, and yielded up their bodies so as*
> *not to serve or worship any god except their own*
> *God"* (Dn 3:28).

His response went further than just words of praise. He decreed that any person who spoke offensively against this God would be torn apart. Shadrach, Meshach, and Abednego again prospered.

The King's Second Dream

After his response of acknowledging God, the king lived in peace in his household and he flourished. However, he then had a dream that made him fearful.

"Now these were the visions [chezev] *in my mind as I lay on my bed: I was looking, and behold, there was a tree in the midst of the earth and its height was great. The tree grew large and became strong And its height reached to the sky, And it was visible to the end of the whole earth. Its foliage was beautiful and its fruit abundant, And in it was food for all. The beasts of the field found shade under it, And the birds of the sky dwelt in its branches, And all living creatures fed themselves from it. I was looking in the visions* [chezev] *in my mind as I lay on my bed, and behold, an angelic watcher, a holy one, descended from heaven. He shouted out and spoke as follows: "Chop down the tree and cut off its branches, Strip off its foliage and scatter its fruit; Let the beasts flee from under it And the birds from its branches. Yet leave the stump with its roots in the ground, But with a band of iron and bronze around it In the new grass of the field; And let him be drenched with the dew of heaven, And let him share with the beasts in the grass of the earth. Let his mind be changed from that of a man And let a beast's mind be given to him, And let seven periods of time pass over him. This sentence is*

of the angelic watchers And the decision d of the holy ones, In order that the living w That the Most High is ruler over the realm of mankind, And bestows it on whom he wishes And sets over it the lowliest of men" (Dn 4:10–17).

President Bush.

Before Daniel gave the interpretation, the king acknowledged that Daniel was *"able, for a spirit of the holy gods is in you"* (v. 18). Daniel expounded on the interpretation (see Dn 4:19–27). Verse 27 holds the key message of the dream:

> *Therefore, O king, may my advice be pleasing to you: break away now from your sins by doing righteousness and from your iniquities by showing mercy to the poor, in case there may be a prolonging of your prosperity* (Dn 4:27).

The dream was given as a warning of what would happen if the king did not turn away from his sin. God was also gracious in telling him how to do that; he was to do righteousness and show mercy to the poor. If the king responded appropriately to the dream, there would be a prolonging of his prosperity. The corollary to this is that, if he did not respond appropriately, there would be no prolonging to his prosperity.

We teach that the interpretation of symbols in our dreams should be simple and personal, and it may cause you to wonder what connection a king with the stature of Nebuchadnezzar would have with a tree. There is a correlation in that one of the seven wonders of the world, the hanging gardens of Babylon, was built by him for his wife. For the years this project took to complete, he would have been very involved in the horticultural details including the selection of its trees.

The King's Response

Only twelve months later, the king was on his roof admiring himself in all his accomplishments as he looked out over great Babylon. His pride was evidence he had not responded appropriately to the dream. Immediately, as the words of his self-praise fell from his mouth, a voice came from heaven saying:

> *"This is what is decreed for you, King Nebuchadnezzar: Your royal authority has been taken from you. You will be driven away from people and will live with the wild animals; you will eat grass like cattle. Seven times will pass by for you until you acknowledge that the Most High is sovereign over the kingdoms of men and gives them to anyone he wishes"* (Dn 4:32).

For seven years, God removed the king from people. He ate grass like an animal. He was wet with dew, and all God had said was fulfilled.

The King's Next Response

At the end of the seven years, King Nebuchadnezzar lifted his head toward heaven and his sound mind returned. He acknowledged, praised, and honored God. The king went through a great restoration period, after which God returned to him the kingdom with majesty and splendor. Men of position began to seek him again, and his greatness was restored to higher levels than he had known before. King Nebuchadnezzar had learned a vital life lesson. In verse 37, he declares:

> *"Now I, Nebuchadnezzar, praise, exalt and honor the King of heaven, for all His works are true and His ways just, and He is able to humble those who walk in pride."*

Summary of Responses to Dreams

Looking at the events in Daniel 2–4, let us learn what we can about responses to dreams.

- *Chose your friends carefully.* The king's first approach was to seek the counsel of his sorcerers, the conjurers, the magicians, and the Chaldeans—the "New Age" experts of his day. Even today, New Age writers present themselves as experts in the understanding of dreams, but only those who feared the Lord, such as Daniel and his friends, were able to help.

- *Seek the support of other believers in praying to God for answers.* Daniel's response to the threat of death was to ask the king for extra time, and then he returned to his friends who also feared God. Together, they requested the compassion of God for the dream and the interpretation so they would not be destroyed.

- *Praise and honor of God is an appropriate response to a dream.* Daniel had a vision/dream in which he received revelation of the king's dream and its interpretation. When he received the night vision of the king's dream, he blessed the God of heaven, acknowledging him publicly to be the source of knowledge and wisdom.

- *Worship will be a response to dreams.* When King Nebuchadnezzar finally received a revelation of God, he fell to his face giving homage briefly to Daniel and then worshiped God, declaring him the God of gods and the Lord of kings and the one who reveals mysteries.

- *Inappropriate responses can misuse dreams.* God gave King Nebuchadnezzar the dream of the multi-layered statue that started with a head of gold and changed to less important metals, down to an iron and clay mixture at the feet. King Nebuchadnezzar misused the idea of the statue and built a real image of himself made wholly of gold and commanded all people to bow in worship of his image.

- *An appropriate response to dreams can yield peace and prosperity.* Following the miracle of Shadrach, Meshach, and Abednego coming safely out of the fire, King Nebuchadnezzar acknowledged their God. Subsequently, King Nebuchadnezzar experienced a time of peace, and he and his kingdom flourished because of his proper praise response.

- *Repentance and restitution are vital responses to dreams.* In the dream of the tree, the Lord warned King Nebuchadnezzar of his sin and even laid out the actions required of him. The dream was clear in describing what would happen to him and to his kingdom if he did not turn from sin, do righteousness, and show mercy to the poor.

- *Timing is important in responding to a dream.* King Nebuchadnezzar let twelve months pass without responding to the dream. Is there an end to God's patience?

- *Issues of our heart can influence responses.* Twelve months later, the king was overlooking his kingdom. He felt very big and secure as he was proclaiming his

149

own praises. Pride had taken root in him and was flourishing. How short was his memory as to the reason for his prosperity!

- *The outcome of inappropriate responses or non-responses can be significant.* Everything God said would happen to the king and his kingdom, did. He lived as a madman for seven years under very adverse conditions, because he did not heed the message of the dream. Even his own people forgot him.

- *Responses of praise are pleasing to God.* As King Nebuchadnezzar merely turned his head toward heaven, his sound mind returned. He began to praise the name of God and give the honor to him once again.

- *Restoration can result from an appropriate response to dreams.* God restored King Nebuchadnezzar's majesty and splendor, and even his kingdom was returned to him in greater measure than before. Even after everything the king had been through at the hand of God, his words expressed that God's ways are true and just and God is able to humble those with pride.

Conclusion

The Bible is the primary source of knowledge and understanding into the ways of our God. When we walk in obedience to him and lift our hearts to him in praise, we will be better equipped to avoid the pitfalls of interpretation and inappropriate responses to dreams—his communication with us.

Chapter Thirteen

Interpretation Pitfalls

$\mathcal{M}$any factors can draw us away from a correct understanding of our dreams. Falling into even one of these "pitfalls" by mistake could make a correct interpretation of our dreams difficult.

In the process of learning, we may make mistakes, but remember this—a mistake is a bigger mistake if we do not learn from it. We will find occasions when we do not get it right, and, with this in mind, we have compiled a few common errors in working though our dreams and helping others with theirs. We found these "pitfalls" because we fell into them ourselves.

Condemnation

Therefore there is now no condemnation for those who are in Christ Jesus (Rom 8:1).

If the dream is a message from the Lord, any interpretation of it must comply with the Word of God. This verse in Romans gives us a primary principle in understanding our dreams. Do not let the enemy use a dream to bring us under condemnation. As a message from the Father, dreams do not condemn, they inform.

> **Dreams do not condemn, they inform.**

No Fear

As another primary principle, what is the first thing spoken to people who have received a visitation by a heavenly being?

> *Then he said to me, "Do not be afraid, Daniel, for from the first day that you set your heart on understanding this and on humbling yourself before your God, your words were heard, and I have come in response to your words"* (Dn 10:12).

> *The angel said to her, "Do not be afraid, Mary; for you have found favor with God"* (Lk 1:30).

Many more references tell us not to fear. This, too, should be a guide in our response to dreams. If the dream brings fear, question its source or your interpretation.

Frustration

One of the quickest ways of not coming to an understanding of a dream is to let ourselves get frustrated. If the meaning of a dream is very important, we can rest assured God will know how to communicate it to us. So relax and set it aside for awhile! One intention of our Father is to be close to his children. Dreams should draw us closer to him, the Giver of dreams. Enjoy the process.

Spending Time on Wrong Dreams

As we have pointed out, not all dreams are from God. Some dreams come to us because of the events of a busy day: *"For a dream* [chalom] *cometh through the multitude of business..."* (Eccl 5:3 KJV).

Time and experience will help us to see the symbolism of our dreams and know which are significant. We talk about clarity, a word we use to differentiate between our dreams, to know which deserve to be written down. God teaches order and structure. Dreams that fail to show these are set aside. Read through the dreams and visions listed in chapter 4 under the heading, "A List of Bible Dreams and Visions," to get an idea of the clarity and structure of those dreams. We use this as a gage for classifying our dreams.

Not Keeping It Simple

The old adage, "Keep it Simple, *Students*" (KISS), holds true here as well. If the interpretation becomes complicated, we may very well have missed the message.

Dream: I was in a house with others. There was a knock at the door. I went to the door. A man handed me some flowers. Later the same thing happened. This happen four or five times. Then I woke up.

What could this possibly mean? It is simple. The dream came on Valentine's Day. The Father was simply expressing his affection for me (Dianne). The repetition was for emphasis.

153

Not Understanding Exaggeration

Dreams will usually over-emphasize something to make a point. Knowing death is impending in a dream does not mean the dreamer is soon going to die unless God appears to tell that individual so. The real meaning is more likely to represent harm or injury and usually emotional or spiritual injury rather than physical. We have likely used or heard children use a phrase like, "My brother is going to kill me when I get home!" I dare say, not many of us would consider calling the police to prevent that killing, because we recognize it as exaggeration to make a point.

Repetition in a dream, another form of exaggeration, lends certainty to an event.

> *Now as for the repeating of the dream to Pharaoh twice, it means that the matter is determined by God, and God will quickly bring it about* (Gn 41:32).

Who is the Dream For?

Dream: I went to the side door and found my wife lying outside. She was on the grass beside the driveway. Bees covered her. I was about to rush out to help her when I realized I needed protection for myself from the bees. I was running around looking for some protection when I woke up.

This is an interesting and short dream I (Steve) had. I shared it with Dianne. As you can imagine, it caused us some concern. We began to pray immediately about the "bees" that had attacked and covered Dianne. We were asking the Lord to show us why they were attacking her.

This was our position on the dream for almost a year, recalling it from time to time in prayer. While reviewing other dreams, I realized my error. It is easy to err in emotion just after having a dream. The dream was for me, not for Dianne. It was about me, not Dianne. How does this apply? If, in this dream, I had only been observing what was happening to Dianne, the dream could have been about Dianne. However, I was very active in the dream. The dream was actually telling me I was not prepared to assist if Dianne was ever in a position of needing my help. The dream was pointing out my need to always be prepared with the proper protective covering (perhaps the armor of God) for a time of need in Dianne's life.

Acting Too Quickly

Every matter must be established by the testimony of two or three witnesses (2 Cor 13:1, NIV).

We must wait until we have a second or third witness before acting on the message of a dream. I (Steve) once woke from a wonderful dream, and before I could say a word, Dianne said, "You had a dream." When I asked how she knew she told me her dream told her I was having a significant dream. We were both in awe at God's love and grace.

Some dreams have obvious clarity and urgency. I do not expect Joseph waited for confirmation from Mary or others before moving with Jesus to Egypt. There was clarity and urgency in the dream. It required immediate action.

Confusing Dream Types

An estimated 95 percent of our message dreams are subjective—for ourselves only. The simplest way to know the difference is to note the activity of the dreamer in the dream. If you are an active participant, the dream is very likely for you (subjective). If you, the dreamer, are only watching the dream unfold, it is likely not about you (objective).

The pitfall we draw attention to here is that we be careful in approaching others that appear in dreams. When we understand a dream is about ourselves (subjective), we seldom cause others problems. When a dream that is for us is taken to be for others (objective), we can cause problems by approaching them if we have not fully understood the interpretation. God does hold us responsible for our actions.

For the objective dream, pray for direction and confirmation that the Father really does want us to approach someone or our church about the dream. It is more likely God has used them in our dream not because the dream is for them, but rather, because they are representative of some characteristic or relationship important to the message of the dream. I (Steve) have often had dreams that included an older brother whom I respected. I know him to represent Jesus in my dreams. My sister, Anna, represents grace; that is what her name means. An older sister represents the Holy Spirit in my dreams. I do not approach them thinking the dream is for them.

The objective dream may be directing us to intercede for the people in the dream or for their situation. If you feel so inclined or directed, pray for them. I assure you that we never do wrong by praying, privately, for the people in our dreams. God is very careful about the privacy of our relationships with him and seldom gives information about someone else.[73]

There are times when the message of a dream may be for someone else, but we must be very careful in these cases. Please walk this path carefully. It is a very serious matter. Much damage can result in spite of good intentions. The flesh can run rampant with potential power. Search your heart for love and humility before doing anything. If the dream is believed to be for a church, the first one to share it with is the pastor of that church and, having done that, follow the pastor's directive. If the dream is from God and he directs us not to share it, the responsibility is with the pastor and no longer ours to carry; release it. It is very important we walk in obedience to those God has placed in authority over us.

There can be a prophetic element to dreams.

> *He said, "Hear now My words: If there is a prophet among you, I, the LORD, shall make Myself known to him in a vision* [marah]. *I shall speak with him in a dream* [chalom]" (Nm 12:6).

Joel 2:28 also associates prophesy with dreams and visions. I believe there are two aspects at work that should not be confused. Everyone dreams or is capable of dreaming; therefore, there may be a personal or subjective aspect to God's communication to them. For those with a prophetic office or gift, there may be a broader, objective aspect to their dreams. In other words,

> It is very important we walk in obedience to those God has placed in authority over us.

those without the prophetic call usually receive only dreams that communicate a personal message to, and for, themselves. Those with a prophetic call may also receive dreams that pertain to the Church, its edification, encouragement, and exhortation.

Prayerfully consider your place in the Church. And as Paul exhorts:

Pursue love, yet desire earnestly spiritual gifts, but especially that you may prophesy (1 Cor 14:1).

The Church today needs those gifted in prophecy as it did in Paul's day. The Church also needs each member to grow to maturity and to walk in love. We are his workmanship, but this work is a cooperative effort. This is very clear in chapter 16, "Dreams and Inner Healing." As the Father shows us issues in our lives, our hearts, and our relationships, we have the option and privilege of taking these issues to him for healing. Dreams are proving to be one method the Father uses to communicate these issues to us and to the Church for the sake of his kingdom.

Do Not Get Logical

A dream is a dream. It is often totally illogical. To try to apply logic to a dream will lead us into the far reaches of nowhere. So, we should not get logical with our dreams, but set logic aside and let the dream's message speak to us.

Avoid Pride

An attitude of pride can sneak up on us unaware! Because dreams come while we sleep, we can do nothing to start or stop them, nor can we do anything to deserve or earn them. We receive dreams from God because he loves us and chooses to have a relationship with us. Pride will sour everything he wants to do in our lives. When we find pride creeping up on us, it is best to confess it as sin, and ask him to remove it from our lives.

Conclusion

As we grow in our understanding of dreams, it is important to have those who can walk with us in times of uncertainty—by watching, teaching, correcting, and encouraging us along the way—helping us avoid the pitfalls of interpretation.

It is valuable to learn all we can by reading and sharing with others who are interested in this wonderful source of relationship with our Father. Get as much experience as you can by interpreting your own dreams. The practice and persistence will pay off.

Chapter Fourteen

Dream Interpretation

*I*n this chapter, we discuss two dreams presented to us during seminars which we worked through as a group. When talking about others' dreams, we are always careful in presenting the meanings of the symbols to the dreamer, as we know the correct understanding of these symbols belongs to the dreamer.

First Dream

A Christian woman, Jane (not her real name), came to us with this dream. It was disturbing to her and she was interested in understanding the meaning. We agreed to work through the details of the dream with her in a way that would show how she could approach her dreams in the future. She shared the following with us:

Dream: In my dream, I was in an institutional type building with grey concrete walls. The building was very square in

that every room was flat-walled. Everywhere I looked, I saw corners, walls, and stairs that led nowhere. Each dimension had been squared off with sharp corners.

Words cannot accurately describe what I saw. There was nothing warm about the place at all. It was grey and empty of furniture, carpets, rugs, and plants. There was nothing there.

As I walked through this building, I knew I was not alone; someone was with me wherever I went but I cannot remember who it was. Then I noticed there was a gate at every outside doorway. These gates were made of tubular metal. They were only small gates running across the centers of the doorways. A person could easily crawl under or climb over them because they touched neither the ground nor the top of the doorway.

There were also large chains around the gates as if they wanted to keep people out or in. I thought this was somewhat stupid. Why put chains on the gates when all a person had to do was to climb over or under to get out? Looking through the doorways, I could see green trees, mountains, and sunshine. It was very inviting. However, there was a bit of fear because of the gates and chains, and I and whoever was with me were trying to escape.

The following describes how we walked Jane through an understanding of the dream.

First, because Jane was a participant in the dream, and not an observer, we recognized it as a subjective dream. Then we wrote out all the symbols found in the dream and included

Dream type = Subjective	
Symbol	*Meaning*
building (institutional)	
walls (bare, gray)	
rooms (square, many, empty)	
stairs (going nowhere)	
someone with her	
gates (short, chains)	
trees, mountains, sunshine	
feeling of fear	
wanting to escape	

the descriptive words or terms used with the symbols. We used the tabular form, as you have seen in chapter 9, to organize the information. We included the second column, to which the meanings were added while we worked through some questions. Sometimes a symbol may have more than one meaning. If all the meanings are listed, the correct one may become evident in walking though the process. We also encourage participants to include any emotions felt during the dreams—impressions, things they "just knew" but did not see or hear, any people, colors and numbers. Many times, we find there is a person in the dream who we somehow know is there even though we cannot see the person or his or her presence is vague. If there is a good feeling or a comfort associated with that person's presence, we believe it may be Jesus.

Before we jumped into the process of identifying the possible meaning of each of the images, we needed information in two areas. We needed to know some things about Jane, and we needed to know the context of the dream.

The Person

Because the meaning of the images is very personal, we cannot understand them correctly apart from knowing the person to some degree. Only Jane has full access to her past memories. Therefore, at best, we could only guide her in the direction of understanding the meaning of the images. This we did by asking questions often derived initially from the dream itself. Obviously, asking what type of car she drove did not appear to have relevance to this dream. So we started our questions by asking Jane what she did for a living. Jane worked as a secretary in a construction company. When we asked her what type of construction the company did, she said, "We build institutional buildings." As she said this, she gave a boisterous laugh. That "obvious" association had eluded her until that moment. This is often the case, especially if frustration sets in. When this association was made, it was a "moment of understanding." This fact was very likely the key to understanding the rest of the dream. We continued to ask her questions focusing on her job. Jane told us, "I like the work but I am frustrated by the environment."

We now begin the transition into the context of the dream.

The Context

The context of the dream related to current events in Jane's life at the time of the dream. We directed our questions to those events. Jane shared that her recent frustration was related to her creative nature and interests as compared to the clerical, repetitive nature of her job. She had been considering a job change but was not sure she could risk it at that time. As she shared these issues, the meaning of the images became clear.

Dream type = Subjective	
Symbol	*Meaning*
Building (institutional)	The job
Walls (bare, gray)	Lack of fulfillment
Rooms (square, many, empty)	Lack of fulfillment
Stairs (going nowhere)	Lack of fulfillment
Someone with her	Jesus is with her
Gates (short, chains)	Things holding her in job
Trees, mountains, sunshine	Real desires
Feeling of fear	Anxiety at job change
Wanting to escape	Wanting to fulfill desires

The Meaning

It seems Jesus was walking with Jane in the dream. The dream was pointing out how boring and sterile the job was to her. The images of green trees and mountains were calling to her creative interests. The dream was showing her how "stupid" the gates were that kept her in that job. One could easily climb over or under the gate. The chains, symbolic of being bound, were shown to be as ridiculous as were the gates. Jane had only to make the decision to change; she was the only thing keeping her in the present job.

The Purpose

Now that we have an understanding of the dream, what is its purpose? Jane already knew a large part of the message of the dream—she was bored and unfulfilled in her job. She shared these details with us during the questioning phase. She also told us the fears she carried at the prospects of a career change. With those details in mind, the real purpose of the dream would seem to be to give her assurance and comfort. It brought assurance and comfort that Jesus was aware of her situation, walking with her, would continue to do so regardless of her decision, and that he would stay with her in that building or "escape" with her should she choose to do so. This is an important point—the final decision on what action to take rested with her.

None of the issues of assurance and comfort are new. They are biblical truths.[74] The dream did not add or take away from those truths, but it did give Jane a very personal experience to associate with them.

Second Dream

A young Christian, Alice (not her real name), presented us with this dream which she had had about two years earlier but had not been able to put out of her mind. It is usually best to work with current dreams because the context details are more vivid, making the interpretation clearer.

Dream: In this dream, I was in a hospital ward filled with casualties. I was dressed like a Catholic priest with the collar and all. My older brother was there with me, though I do not recall him doing or saying anything much, just helping me with what I was doing. The casualties were on beds lined up next to each other as in an intensive care unit.

Some were conscious and physically able to respond to human interaction.

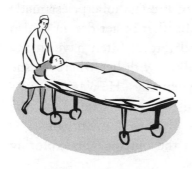

I was going to each bed, asking the individuals if they knew Jesus as their Lord and Savior, if they knew where they were going to spend eternity, and if they wanted me to pray with them. Those who rejected my approach I left and went to the next bed.

Some responded with gratitude, while others were hostile toward me. In the name of Jesus, I was casting out demons, healing the sick, and leading others to the Lord.

The Person

Alice was a young single woman in one of our seminars. She had had the dream while she was still a student. Presently, she was working as a secretary.

The Context

At the time of the dream, Alice was involved in an evangelism team with her church.

The Meaning

As we worked our way through the symbolism in her dream, the issue of the Catholic priest came to the fore. Alice was concerned because she was not Catholic. When we asked her what a minister in her denomination would wear, she said it would likely be shorts and a T-shirt. Then we asked her if she, in the dream, had been wearing shorts and a T-shirt, would she recognize herself as being in a position of leadership? She admitted the association would not be there. The dream needed some way of symbolizing leadership, and the garments of the Catholic priest made that association possible. The brother in her dream is also an interesting image and one I (Steve) often have in my dreams. The older brother walked with her wherever she went but did not take over the activities. He was not over-bearing or undermining. Jesus so wonderfully fits the image it is usually immediately obvious in my dreams.

The following chart shows the outcome of exploring the symbols in Alice's dream.

The Purpose

We felt the dream was a vocation dream, pointing Alice in the direction the Lord had for her life. The dream was suggesting she was gifted in evangelism and healing. We suggested she pray about this calling, asking the Lord to confirm his direction for her life in other ways before she

Dream type = Subjective	
Symbol	*Meaning*
hospital ward	sick people
intensive care	last chance
brother	Jesus
Catholic priest	leadership
healing sick	healing
casting out demons	routine Christian ministry
leading to the Lord	evangelism

took any action herself. We discussed the differences between "calling" and "commissioning" and that there would likely be a period of training through which the Lord would take her before she was commissioned. We admired her willingness to follow the Lord wherever he led her.

What to Do With a Dream

* Write the dream down as soon as possible after you receive it!

"Jesu, what is the meaning of --- ? "

* Ask the Giver of dreams for understanding.

* Read the dream over again.

* Work through the dream as we did above or find a trusted listener—one who can guide with questions without imposing a meaning onto it.

* Pray over the obvious details of the dream if the meaning remains elusive, and be prepared to leave it in God's hands. Later, events may bring some insight into the meaning.

* Review your dreams from time to time. Develop your own dictionary of dream symbols and pictures. You will find understanding comes more effortlessly as you invest in them.

* Trust the Father and leave the dream with him, especially if things remain unclear. It may be a matter of timing. Again, answers may be clear later.

Questions to Aid in Interpretation

These are some of the questions you, as the dreamer, could ask yourself. Write your answers in a chart for clarity.

* What is your role in the dream? Is it observing, participating, or active? This helps to identify the type of

dream—objective or subjective (described in chapter 7). If you are an active participant in the dream, it is about you and not about the other people in it. Look for the role you play as the drama unfolds.

- What symbols are presented as important or significant? List, on paper, the symbols in your dream along with the action or descriptive words associated with those objects. Ask yourself what they mean to you, what emotion or characteristic about them stands out.

- What features stand out as important? A color, texture, or size? These are important descriptions. Especially pay attention to things heard or read on signs or notes.

- Reduce the dream to its simplest form. Find the central message, the main theme.

The Moment of Understanding

The moment of understanding is when something clicks—a light comes on. There seems to be a witness in our spirit that we have found the meaning or are on the path to finding it. In our first example, this came when Jane associated the building in the dream with the place where she worked. When this moment of understanding comes, something in us says "yes!" A favored verse of ours is: *"Let the peace of Christ rule* [brabeuo] *in your hearts"* (Col. 3:15). The word *brabeuo* translated here as "rule" is interesting. Its literal meaning is "to act as umpire." It tells us to let the peace of Christ act as an umpire in our hearts, helping us to know right and wrong. If peace is not there or leaves, look for foul play; if peace remains, it was a fair play.

So when the "moment of understanding" comes, check to see if there is peace within and, if there is, go with that answer.

Conclusion

It is very important we do not impose a meaning onto someone else's dream. For that reason, we would not like to publish a dictionary of dream symbols. We have included a brief list of common symbols in chapter 10 but ask you to view this list only as a guide for how symbols and pictures could be used or understood. As evident in our examples, the context or events in the life of the dreamer at the time of the dream are extremely important in understanding the dream. Equally important are the meaning and relevance of the symbols to the dreamer. Each person has their own life history through which the Father speaks to them, so they alone can know the meaning at the moment when "the light" comes on.

Part III

Caring...

"Jesus said to him, "Tend My sheep.""

John 21:17

Chapter Fifteen

Leaders and the Dreamer

elationship is paramount to the Kingdom of God. His command is that we love one another as he has loved us. While the irresponsible actions of a dreamer can affect much damage to a body of believers, shepherds also, on occasion, wound sheep.

I therefore, the prisoner of the Lord, entreat you to walk in a manner worthy of the calling with which you have been called, with all humility and gentleness, with patience, showing forbearance to one another in love, being diligent to preserve the unity of the Spirit in the bond of peace (Eph 4:1).

Much of the damage, whether by member or by leader, can be attributed to a lack of understanding.

My people are destroyed for lack of knowledge. Because you have rejected knowledge, I also will reject you from being My priest (Hos 4:6).

The price for rejecting knowledge is very high. Understanding and knowledge begin with the fear of the Lord and increase with study and learning; both are activities required of leaders. We are more likely to be afraid of things we know little or nothing about. By reading this book, you have 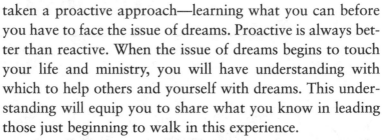 taken a proactive approach—learning what you can before you have to face the issue of dreams. Proactive is always better than reactive. When the issue of dreams begins to touch your life and ministry, you will have understanding with which to help others and yourself with dreams. This understanding will equip you to share what you know in leading those just beginning to walk in this experience.

We talked about the likelihood that those new to the reality of dreams would make mistakes, as new babies learning to walk. Whether the dreamer or a leader to the dreamer, we are subject to mistakes. The damage is minimized when we walk together with understanding, knowing what lies

> Proactive is always better than reactive.

ahead, directing those we are helping around the dangers, and always encouraging them to walk.

Not all of the damage that results is the fault of the leader or the dreamer. An old adage says, "the truth hurts" and suggests sometimes the hearer is responsible for the damage by their reaction to the message of the dream or the dreamer. This is the subject of chapter 16, "Dreams and Inner Healing." As leaders, we need the wisdom of Solomon and the courage of Nathan the prophet to face, defuse, and correct those times when people are hurt by the actions of others. The following are two examples of real situations of responses to dreams and dreamers.

Please Hear Me

A friend gifted in the prophetic was experiencing dreams. As her understanding grew, she came to know which dreams were personal and which were given as messages for her church. Her church was a source of excitement for her because the people there were open to the things of the Spirit. She believed this fellowship would help her grow in her prophetic gift.

There were good relationships between herself and the members, the leaders, and the pastor. She was faithful in attendance. In time, she started having dreams she believed were for the leadership of the church. After recording one of these, she made an appointment with the pastor to discuss the dream. (We are not so interested in the actual dream in this chapter but more in the interaction between pastor and dreamer.) After she had shared the dream, his response surprised her. He dismissed it with the comment, "It was only a dream." In discouragement, she left the meeting, not knowing what to do except to pray for the leadership of the church.

She continued to have dreams she felt were for the leadership of this church. Another dream, in particular, motivated her to make another appointment with her pastor. Again, she brought this new dream to him. Sadly, his response was much the same as before. The pastor listened but dismissed this one as well.

After the third and last attempt to share a new dream with the pastor, she again left discouraged, but this time with finality. Although she had followed due processes and had prayed for the leadership, she felt belittled and ignored. Despite her relationship with many in this church, including several of the leaders, she felt the time had come to leave and to worship with another part of the body of Christ. A short time later, this church was dissolved, and the people were left to find other churches.

Although there are many factors that contribute to the demise of a church, we are moved by the thought that this closure might have been prevented had the response of the pastor been different.

The Youth Leader

Many years ago when I (Dianne) was beginning my discovery of the gift of dreams in my life, I had a dream. In my dream was the youth leader of the church I had belonged to for a number of years. I pondered the dream for a while, eventually believing I was to share it with him. It was Friday night, and I knew the youth of our church would be at the church office, so I drove to the office. They were near the end of the prayer ministry time, and I quietly approached the young man. I told him I had a dream I felt was for him and would like to relate it to him. We went to a quiet place, and I shared the dream as I had written it down. (Again, in this chapter we are focusing on the relationship between the leader and the dreamer rather than the actual dream.) He listened and thought about it. After a few minutes, he said it did not particularly mean anything to him now, but he would like to take my written copy and spend some time praying about and pondering it. He expressed appreciation at my coming to meet with him and was impressed by my desire to be obedient to what the Lord had asked me to do. I then offered to pray with him. With obvious enthusiasm, he accepted. Others joined us and we spent about thirty-five minutes praying for him. The dream never came up again after that meeting. The important point in all this for me was that I left the church office that night feeling encouraged, obedient, and full of the joy of living for God. I was excited about this gift and the thought that God would speak to me in dreams.

In this situation, the youth leader proved receptive. He was able to work with the dreamer, to encourage the dreamer, and to maintain or strengthen her self-esteem. In doing so, he ensured she would be open to receive advice and direction from him in the future.

The Picnic

One night, I (Dianne) had a dream that was incredibly clear and very impressive in its power and potential. When I woke up, I did not know the meaning. I wrote it out and shared it with Steve as follows:

Dream: There was a big pond. I was beside it. The ground began to tremble. I climbed up some rocks and turned to look over the pond. As the trembling of the ground increased, I saw a tremendous stirring of the water to form a powerful upsurge that formed a very huge, strong, almost solid column of water. The water around the base of the column remained calm. It went very high, and when my eye followed it to the top, I could see a very large plane that had just taken off, heading up into the sky. It was right at the point of being in line with the top of the water column.

We had no clear insight into the meaning but noted that, in the main part of the dream, I was an observer. Weeks went by, and I pondered the dream and prayed about it without having much insight. Then, one day, we were enjoying a Sunday drive in the countryside with the director of a large para-church organization and his wife. We had stopped for a break at a place overlooking the ocean, enjoying both the scenery and the fellowship, when the dream suddenly came to my mind. I wondered why and sat quietly listening for a few minutes. I began to get the impression the Lord wanted to speak to this couple and that, perhaps, the dream had been for them. I asked the Lord for an opportunity to speak with them if this was correct. I then waited, trusting the Lord.

Lunchtime was a picnic at the edge of the water on a beautiful sunny day. The conversation centered on what the Lord was doing in our lives, and this gave me the opportunity I needed to share the dream. The husband began to share some insights from the Lord concerning future directions but was not sure how these might work out. I asked him to hold his information to see if the dream might confirm what the Lord was doing. I related the dream. The husband's response began with teary eyes and silence until he could regain some strength in his voice. The dream had spoken to his heart, and the result was a wonderful time of sharing from our hearts. Each of us felt the presence and love of God that day.

Submitting Dreams to Leaders

> *Every person is to be in subjection to the governing authorities. For there is no authority except from God, and those which exist are established by God. Therefore whoever resists authority has opposed the ordinance of God; and they who have opposed will receive condemnation upon themselves* (Rom 13:1–2).

Let us summarize some points that we feel dreamers should consider in submitting an objective dream to leadership.

- Write the dream down just as it came to you. Do not embellish. Pray, pray and pray some more until you have an assurance in your spirit to approach leadership. God's timing is important.

- Call and ask for a time to meet. Do not approach leadership on a Sunday morning or while their mind is on an event in the present.

- When asking for an appointment, let them know that it is regarding a dream. This saves the 'fretting' that some people go through if they are kept in the dark regarding the subject of a meeting.

- At the meeting, keep it simple. Just give the dream to the leader. Remember that an objective dream is about and for others. You may not have the meaning of the dream. Say as little as possible and let the Holy Spirit speak to the heart of the leader.

- You are not responsible for what the leader does with the dream—you have done your part. Do not judge nor get hurt by their response regardless of what you hoped for.

- Following the meeting, speak no more about the dream unless asked by the leader. This is especially important if time passes and you do not see the changes you thought you would see. Your responsibility is done. Do not 'remind' the leader of your dream.

- We are always to honor authority. This gives room for God to work.

Receiving From Dreamers

Therefore, I exhort the elders among you ... shepherd the flock of God among you, exercising oversight not under compulsion, but voluntarily, according to the will of God; and not for sordid gain, but with eagerness; nor yet as lording it over those allotted to your charge, but proving to be examples to the flock (1 Peter 5:1–3).

Let us summarize some points we feel leaders should consider when receiving from dreamers under their care.

- Give time to the dreamer. Be open to meet with him or her.

- Listen and affirm. The time you give should be worthy of the excitement and anxiety they went through making the appointment to see you.

- Respond with interest. This person is one of God's children and in your care.

- Look at the person as they speak. Make eye contact. Do not let paperwork or phone calls distract you.

- Ask questions for clarity. Having the material from this book will put you in a better position to ask quality questions about subjective/objective dreams.

- Express sincere appreciation for their courage to come to you, for their desire to grow in a gift given them by God, for their heart of obedience, and for the gracious submission of their dream to the proper channels of authority.

- When the dream has been shared, pray, with the dreamer, for understanding.

- If you are not sure about the appropriateness of the

dream for you or your church, ask them to leave the dream with you to pray about it. If you tell them you will contact them in a set number of days, do so.

- Pray about the dream and share it with one or two other leaders (keeping the name of the dreamer to yourself so they hear the dream without first evaluating the source), asking for their insights.

- If you believe the dreamer has misunderstood the subjective/objective nature of the dream, teach them to know the difference. Suggest material for further study and offer to meet with them to discuss this further if necessary.

- Leave the door open for future possibilities. One never knows what God will do next.

Responding to a Dreamer

My friend, Norma, shared a dream with me (Dianne) over coffee. As a pastor, you may well be faced with a scenario like this. How might you respond? How should you respond? The following is a simple approach that will build up rather than discourage. She sat across the table from me and recounted the dream as follows:

Dream: In the dream, I feel sad and oppressed. The Lord shows me a house with two dogs in it (dogs and animals lift me up). There is a scene change, and now I am trying to find the house with the two dogs. I cannot find it. I tell God I cannot find it. He shows me the house. One dog comes out and then a second dog comes out. I see a priest sitting down. I ask him, "How many dogs are there?" He tells me there are twenty-six.

Following a "repeat after me" style of prayer, we prayed together. I prayed, "Jesus, why could I not find the house?"

Norma repeated those same words. Jesus answered her, saying, "It was beyond your reasoning." Norma looked up and smiled as she shared his answer with me.

I prayed, and she repeated, "Jesus, what is the meaning of the first dog?" Jesus answered, "Purity." Norma got teary as she shared that answer.

And so we continued: "Jesus, what is the meaning of the second dog?" "Truth." She began to cry.

"Jesus, what is the significance of the priest?" "Counsel." She understood Jesus to be her counselor. She also understood that Jesus is our high priest and now her high priest in a more personal way.

"Jesus, who is the priest?" "Your friend." She knew in her spirit it was Jesus.

"Jesus, what is the meaning of twenty-six dogs?" "Happiness." Norma's eyes filled again.

"Jesus, what is your encouraging word to me today?" "Go in peace." Tears of joy came and she cried.

"Jesus, what is the overall meaning of this dream?" "It is for your comfort."

Norma told me this dream was an answer to many prayers with regard to herself. She struggled much with condemnation and often asked the Lord, "How am I doing?" The Father used this dream to answer her question. He brought Norma assurance that she is doing just fine, and the dream resulted in bringing her comfort and peace. She also felt the Lord was saying of her that her character was one of purity and truth. Overall in her life, Norma admitted being in a place of happiness. Because of this dream, Norma is more confident in her prayer life and in her relationship with him.

This is simple. Try it on the dreamer that comes your

way and see the positive effect it has on you of both. Watch how it builds those who are down, encourages the discouraged, and heals the hurts and wounds of past relationships.

> *And he gave* [you], *for the equipping of the saints for the work of service, to the building up of the body of Christ; until we all attain to the unity of the faith, and of the knowledge of the son of God, to a mature man, to the measure of the stature which belongs to the fullness of Christ.*[75]

Conclusion

The Father created us for relationship and this makes us responsible for our actions toward each other. Our gifts and callings are given for the building up of the body of Christ. Leaders have a special role in this, as shepherds are to lead their sheep, not to scatter them by inappropriate responses. If a dreamer approaches you, how are you now equipped to relate to them? How have you prepared the soil of your heart to properly respond toward the care and feeding of the dreamers in your flock? One way would be to seek inner healing to remove the triggers that so quickly cause problems in our lives and our relationships.

Chapter Sixteen

Dreams and Inner Healing

Relationship

God has created us for relationship. The devil's first and still most successful attack against God is to damage his children's capacity for relationship. When sin came, Adam and Eve hid themselves from each other and from God. The enemy must have been delighted. We can see the effect of this damage in their new-found ability to blame each other and God.[76] Inner healing is being used today to reverse the damage past relationships have caused, and God uses dreams in this process. Jesus, the Wonderful Counselor,[77] is the center of this healing even in our dreams.

Barb's Dream

During one of our dreams and counseling seminars, we asked those attending to submit a dream and to be prepared to go through a counseling session. Barb (not her real name) came to us with a dream. She started to cry as she began to tell this dream:

Dream: In my dream, I was moving. My car was packed full of my baggage. I got a phone call. My friends were at the airport and needed me to pick them up. I drove to my in-laws to drop off my baggage, so I would have room for my friends and their baggage in my car. I went to the airport to pick them up and parked the car. When I returned, a police officer was by my car. He turned to me and told me this was my car. My friends and I left the airport.

Then I found myself at the podium in my church. I was giving my testimony. As I was speaking, a darkness came over and surrounded me. I fell to the floor. As I was lying there, others gathered around me. I saw Bill (my husband). He was holding my baby. The others were telling me to sign the papers giving Bill my baby. I was confused and did not trust them. I did not want Bill to have my baby.

Context

Barb had been under much distress for more than a week, trying to understand the dream. She had been separated from her husband, Bill (not his real name). The last thing she had received from him before the separation was her car, and she had been troubled mentally, wanting to know if she should return the car to him. Another couple had agreed to walk with Barb, helping her through the marriage problems. Even as I describe these context details, I am sure you are beginning to see some of the meaning unfold.

Prayer Counseling

We began the prayer counseling approach to this dream by asking the Lord the meaning of each of the symbols and elements of the dream. As we did so, Barb grew increasingly restless, shaking as she sat there. As we came to the scene where the "darkness" came over and surrounded her, it became more obvious; she was not simply nervous—there was a demonic source. Before continuing with the dream, we led Barb through some prayers of repentance and forgiveness of those involved in her situation and then commanded the demon to go to the feet of Jesus. Her posture and countenance changed immediately as peace returned. The images from the dream showed that the demonic had found "an opening"[78] from which it could rob her of peace. As we continued to pray through the dream, it was wonderful to watch her face light up as Jesus, the Wonderful Counselor, spoke his truth into her situation and expressed his love for her.

This one dream led to two hours of counseling, including a number of counseling side trails on related memories. She had entered the room in fear and under distress; she left the room radiant and full of joy. Weeks later, a follow-up phone call proved she continued to receive comfort from the interpretation of that dream. Jesus is the Wonderful Counselor!

Caution

Be careful in the inner healing ministry, because we often face the enemy in these deep recesses, and they are very reluctant to leave "home." Much damage can result where training and experience in prayer counseling are lacking.

Healing through Dreams

In the preceding chapters, we have presented examples from the Bible showing that God speaks into the lives of people through dreams. In response, these people have given high value to their dreams because they recognized them as communication from God. In the prayer counseling ministry, we are finding that God uses dreams to bring healing to the wounds of people. This restores their capacity for relationship.

Healing Dreams and the Bible

There is often a progression in the way God works. As seen in Job 33:14–18, God loves people so much, he will get their attention one way or another, speaking once or twice. Sadly, often no one listens to it. It is when "sound sleep falls" that God "opens the ears" to seal his instruction. This is a marvelous thing. In the night when we "slumber in our beds," our God sometimes reaches down to speak his truth into our hearts. What is exciting is that this method of speaking bypasses the human need to analyze, figure things out, or control what is happening. Our loving God connects with us—his Spirit to our spirit. His purpose is to *"turn man aside from his conduct, And keep man from pride."* He also desires to *"keep back his soul from the pit, And his life from passing over into Sheol."* Through dreams, God reveals and heals the heart and so saves us from significant consequences.

In chapter 12, "Responding to Dreams," we dealt with one of King Nebuchadnezzar's dreams in Daniel 4:10–17. In this dream, he saw a large tree that was cut down. A band of iron and bronze was placed around the rim of the stump for seven years while the man grazed on grass in the wild. King Nebuchadnezzar suffered that fate one year later. He was given that dream out of mercy in the hope he would repent of the attitude of his heart and so avoid the outcome. This dream can be seen as a warning dream or a prophetic dream, but it could also have been a healing dream if he had acted on it for the correction of the pride that was brewing in his heart.

Peter's heart needed some corrective attention as well. If God had not given him the vision of the sail cloth full of unclean animals (three times), he would not have been in a position to hear the plea of the Gentiles asking him to come to Caesarea. How would the future of the Church have been affected if that vision had not "corrected" a social/relationship concern in Peter's heart? God only knows.

Healing Dreams and Prayer Counseling

As in Peter's case, healing dreams can do their work without the aid of a counselor. However, there may be times when the wounds or circumstances of the dreamer hamper his or her ability to work through the interpretation or hear from the Lord. At these times, a prayer counselor may be required to come alongside and help the dreamer in hearing the Lord, thus assisting in the healing.

The following are a few examples of dreams brought to a counseling session. They began the time of healing.

Pat's Dreams

Pat (not her real name) had requested two full days of prayer counseling at Cornerstone with the director and myself (Dianne). She had carried the hurt long enough. She was ready for some healing! After the usual questions related to her personal history, we asked a casual question: "Have you had any dreams lately?" Pat was surprised by the question but admitted having two dreams just days ago.

191

Dream 1: There was a large aquarium full of water. Two people were telling me to get into it. I was terrified because there was only a little room to breathe and I was claustrophobic. I could not go in.

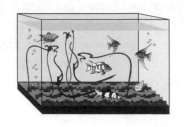

Dream 2: I was at the top of a hill. I began going down the hill. There were rocks on either side of me as I went down. There were also rocks at the bottom. As I went down the hill, there was lots of air, a breeze, and wind all around me. I could breath so easily. I found myself almost running down the hill, feeling free. As I looked toward the bottom, I thought, "So this is what it is like."

After relating those dreams, Pat proceeded to tell us her interpretation. She said we were the two people, her counselors. We were trying to get her into the aquarium, a place she did not want to go. It represented demonic attack.

We asked her to set aside that interpretation until we had a chance to pray through the dream, asking Jesus what things meant.

Healing Prayer

We began to pray into the dream, asking Jesus to take Pat back into her memory of the dream. Then, in a "repeat after me" style of prayer, we began to ask questions of Jesus, and Pat shared his answers with us. The prayer went something like this:

Question: Jesus, what does the aquarium represent?
Answer: It represents my life.
Q. What does it mean that people are encouraging me into the aquarium?

A. Fear.

Q. What does being encouraged to get in mean?

A. There is healing.

Q. What does the little space to breathe mean?

A. This is where you are presently at.

Q. What does my not wanting to go into the aquarium because of being claustrophobic mean?

A. You don't believe I will save you.

Q. Jesus, how do we pray into this dream?

A. Keep praying.

We continued by praying in the same way through the second dream:

Q. Jesus, please explain the second dream.

A. Fresh air and room to breathe.

Q. Jesus, both dreams, how do they compare?

A. Freedom in Jesus.

Q. Jesus, what negative conclusion did I make about myself in the first dream?

A. I am fearful.

Q. In what ways has fearfulness influenced my life?

A. In many ways.

At this point, we had Pat repent and ask forgiveness for the place she had given lies and then prayed destruction to the structure of fear in her life. We then continued in prayer:

Q. Jesus, what is your revelation of truth?

A. Trust in me.

Q. What is your encouraging word to me?

A. Love.

We prayed Pat would embrace and accept this love which was being poured out in place of the fear.

You can see that, with Jesus, there is no formula. The step-by-step procedure for the first dream symbols was not the direction the Lord wanted to go with the second dream. It serves us well to remember there is no ABC method when it comes to Jesus. He will lead in his own unique way, and we are but facilitators working alongside him. But let us continue in this example.

With this method, we walked through the symbols of each dream, asking Jesus what each represented. After extensive ministry, we prayed Pat would accept and embrace the truths she had received from Jesus and that his love would displace the fear that was part of her life.

Significance of Pat's Dreams to Healing

These dreams led into an extensive time of prayer for healing in many areas of Pat's life. On the second day, as the ministry time went on, Pat had to face a difficult choice. There were some memories in the early years of her life into which she did not want to venture. Her dilemma was whether she should quit now and perhaps return later when she might have more courage, or continue now and face those fears. In trying to encourage her to go on, we pointed out that Jesus promised to be with her through it all. We reminded her of the dreams. We walked through them with her again, pointing to the words of truth Jesus had revealed to her:

It is difficult to get into the healing aquarium, but you have encouragers with you. You are currently in a place where there is little room to breathe. If you chose to get in, the "little space to breathe" will transform into lots of air, breeze, and wind where breathing is so easy. As you run down the hill, you will feel free and think, "So this is what it's like to be free."

Reminded of those words, Pat agreed to carry on. These dreams were pivotal to the two days of healing. The Lord Jesus clearly exposed that she had believed some lies that produced fear in her. He spoke his truth into her heart, saying, "Trust in me." He also gave encouragement to Pat by speaking the one word—love—to her. It was a turning point in the ministry time.

These two dreams were given to Pat by God before she even arrived for counseling. We opened the two-day session with Pat's own dreams. These dreams also established the client's confidence in her ability to hear God. Sometimes, people doubt their ability to hear. When she was reminded she had already heard from God through the dreams, the doubt was removed and it convinced her she did have the ability to hear him. This was important to the success of the ministry time.

These dreams also enabled the client to choose to push through a difficult phase of the session. She did experience much healing from Jesus in those two days.

Lucy's Dream

During a counseling session with us, Lucy (not her real name), shared this dream:

Dream: I was tending an old store. There was a back hallway leading to some stairs. Up the stairs, I could hear a radio playing. I was told that the radio was to be kept playing loudly to let people think someone was in the store. The radio seemed not to be working very well. There was some static, and then it went too soft to hear. The store was empty, so I went up the stairs and stumbled around in the dark, trying to find the radio to turn it up louder. After I did so, I hurried downstairs. After a short while, the static started and

the volume went soft. Again, I went up to correct it. This time, I located it quickly; I was gone from the store for just a minute or so. When I did get back, two policemen were there. They said to me, "Lady, you have just been robbed."

Context

Lucy and her husband had just bought a home and she was beginning a new job, not sure what was expected of her in that job.

Prayer Counseling for Lucy

We prayed through the details of the dream with Lucy, asking Jesus what each symbol meant. He spoke to her and she shared her responses with us.

The store represented these major changes in her life—the house and especially the job—for which she had to bear all the responsibility. The Lord exposed her fear, the lie that she would fail to handle the responsibilities that were going to be given her. Jesus brought her this truth—she would be given only what she could handle. He also promised he would give her strength to fulfill tasks. As a final word of encouragement, he told her he was well pleased with her.

Lucy left the session far more relaxed and encouraged. She had learned Jesus was well pleased with her.

Conclusion

These people and many others have been touched by the God who loves them. They leave the counseling time with an improved ability to enter into relationships. In coming days, other wounds in need of attention may surface. We believe the love and mercy of God places us in situations that allow us to see things in our lives that need attention. This is part of our sanctification. This is his work but a work in which we are partners. As we see the effects of the wounds, we have a choice. Do we bring the need to him for healing, or do we continue trying to suppress it, carrying it with us for the rest of our lives? We see repeatedly the love and compassion our God has for his children. We see his interest in the daily activities of their lives. We see his willingness to take their woundedness and set them free. We see the obvious changes in their countenance in the midst of a counseling session. This warrants repeating these words of Scripture:

The Spirit of the Lord GOD is upon me, Because the LORD has anointed me To bring good news to the afflicted; he has sent me to bind up the brokenhearted, To proclaim liberty to captives, And freedom to prisoners; To proclaim the favorable year of the LORD, And the day of vengeance of our God; To comfort all who mourn, To grant those who mourn in Zion, Giving them a garland instead of ashes, The oil of gladness instead of mourning, The mantle of praise instead of a spirit of fainting. So they will be called oaks of righteousness, The planting of the LORD, that He may be glorified. Then they will rebuild the ancient ruins, They will raise up the former devastations, And they will repair the ruined cities, The desolations of many generations. And strangers will stand and pasture your flocks, And foreigners will be your farmers and your vine-dressers. But you will be called the priests of the LORD; You will be spoken of as ministers of our God. You will eat the wealth of nations, And in their riches you will boast. Instead of your shame you will have a double portion, And instead of humiliation they will shout for joy over their portion. Therefore they will possess a double portion in their land, Everlasting joy will be theirs (Is 61:1–7).

Our God is preparing a bride for his son, one without spot or wrinkle. He is a God who has things to say, to share, with his children. He is an awesome God, above all gods. He created us for relationship—especially with him.

Chapter Seventeen

Pleasant Dreams

---

*D*oes God speak through dreams? Are all dreams from God? How do we know which are message dreams and what do we do with them?

These were some of the important questions posed earlier in this book. By examining what the Bible tells us about dreams, we have seen that dreams are very important to God, to the point of entrusting the success of the nation Israel and the life of Jesus, his only son, to dreams. Through the presentation of our own dream experiences and those of others, we have illustrated that God speaks to us today in personal and significant ways through dreams.

Dreams have been defined as a series of images with sounds, emotion, and some seemingly illusive meanings. Will we now be able to understand all our message dreams? Having read this book, we feel confident in saying you have entered into the *process* of better understanding your dreams. It is a process and, as such, requires time, diligence and experience to achieve proficiency. Knowing which dreams are subjective and which are objective is a vital step in understanding the message. The dream language is actually one we have been familiar with from our early years as we learned using symbols and pictures. Metaphors are as common to our everyday lives "as copper pennies." We trust we have raised your awareness to these things and, in doing so, demystified and simplified the process of interpretation of dreams. The dreamer holds the key to interpretation, because the symbols are personalized by God to the uniqueness of each person and often within the context of their lives.

> Some dreams may be given as information only, and only when we arrive at the fulfillment of the dream we realize the meaning and then see how God has been directing events in our lives.

Avoid the "fast food" mentality that you must know the meaning of every dream immediately; as we have observed from those of the Old Testament, understanding and fulfillment often did not come until years later. Some dreams may be given as information only, and only when we arrive at the fulfillment of the dream we realize the meaning and then see how God has been directing events in our life. We have dreams, written down many years ago, that we continue to review, hoping for new understanding or to apply some new insight to the symbols.

Responsibility

Receiving any message from God carries much responsibility. Once we have determined the type of dream we have received, what the message and purpose is, and who it may be for, we have choices to make. What do we do with the dream and its message?

There is one gage against which we must measure our response and our responsibility; that gage is LOVE. We must act within the parameters of love—toward those around us and as well as ourselves. Love is a verb not a noun; it is what we do. Our actions are the measure of love.

> *Love is patient and kind. Love is not jealous or boastful or proud or rude. Love does not demand its own way. Love is not irritable, and it keeps no record of when it has been wronged. It is never glad about injustice but rejoices whenever the truth wins out. Love never gives up, never loses faith, is always hopeful, and endures through every circumstance. Love will last forever, but prophecy and speaking in unknown languages and special knowledge will all disappear. There are three things that will endure— faith, hope, and love—and the greatest of these is love* (1 Cor 13:4–8,13, NLT).

Please review these verses before you do anything with a dream, a vision, or a prophetic word. Do everything with a love motive, just like our Father.

This area of dreams is about him! He is the Giver of dreams and he holds the interpretation of our dreams. It is all about relationship, on a personal and a corporate level, with a God who delights in being Father to his children, a God who wrote the book on being creative, a God who created and uses the concept of communication through dreams with all its wonderful and imaginative symbols and images.

Remember that dreams, as with every aspect of our Christian walk, are about relationship—relationship with the Godhead and with his creation.

Pleasant dreams!

Appendix

KEY WORDS STUDY

The Bible was originally written in the Hebrew and Greek languages (some Aramaic as well). It is sometimes advantageous to study the original language for a more complete understanding of the words used in Scripture.

In chapter 11, we pointed to the importance of context to the meaning of a dream using as an illustration the word "bridge." This principle is equally important in understanding the meaning and intent of the words of the original language. The context of a verse, the Scriptures surrounding the word, gives us a basis for understanding its proper meaning.

Authorship is an important factor in the choice of words used to express a meaning. One author may be writing during a time of exile and influenced by that cultural milieu, while another author includes words specific to his vocation (for example, Amos was a farmer and this is reflected in his writings).

The intended audience also influences the author's use of words in Scripture. One audience may be doing right in the sight of the Lord while another is in need of admonishing. One audience may be in exile and the other at home. The understanding of words and context may vary from one audience to another according to the cultural setting of the audience. Using the Scriptures, let us examine an example of this.

The book of Genesis is full of the word *chalom* as a noun meaning "dream," but the writer in the book of Daniel uses an Aramaic word *chelem* as the noun meaning "dream." Only Matthew uses the word *onar* in his narratives of the birth of Jesus and once in the narrative of the death of Jesus when Pilate's wife has a dream.

Why is one word used frequently in one book of the Bible while a different word is favored in another book? Author style, reader audience, and cultural setting are big reasons for the differences. Even today, languages change and the meaning of words drift out of vogue as with words like "gay" or "pot."

The following is an extensive list of both Hebrew and Greek words for dream/dreams, and vision/visions. Some interesting observations will be made at the end.

Hebrew: Dream/Dreams

חָלַם *chalam* (khaw-lam)[79] verb

1. **to dream:**
    i) of ordinary dreams of sleep (Is 29:8)
    ii) of dreams with prophetic meaning (Gn 28:12; 41:1,5; Jl 2:28; Gn 37:5,6,9,10; 40:5,8)
    iii) of dreams of false prophets (Jer 29:8)

2. **to be healthy, to be strong:**
    i) *Qal*, young are strong as in healthy (Jb 39:4)
    ii) *Hiphil*, restore to health (Is 38:16)

חֲלֹם *chalom* (khal-ome')[80] noun

1. **dream:**
    i) ordinary dream of sleep (Gn 20:3,6; Gn 31:10 [Genesis often uses this word]; Jb 7:14; 20:8; Eccl 5:3,7; Is 29:7)
    ii) dreams with prophetic meaning (Gn 37:5,6,9,10; Gn

40:5,8; Jl 2:28; Dn 2:3). This is also seen of false prophets who had dreams as well and the Israelites were warned against listening to false dreams (Nm 12:6; Dt 13:1,3,5; Jer 23:27,28,32; Zec 10:2).

Our main verse, Joel 2:28, uses both of these words, *chalam, chalom* where it reads: *"shall dream dreams."*

חֲלֶם *chelem* (khay'-lem: Aramaic)[81] noun

1. dream (Dn 2:4,5,6,7,9,26,28,36,45; Dn 5:12; Dn 7:1).

Greek: Dream/Dreams

ὄναρ *onar* (on'-ar)[82] noun

1. dream; only in Matthew (1:20; 2:12,13,19,22; 27:19).

ἐνύπνιον *enupnion* (en-oop'-nee-on)[83] noun

1. dreams.

In Acts 2:17, *enupnion* is the first dream. The Greek actually reads *"dreams will dream."*

ἐνυπνιάζομαι *enupniazomai* (en-oop-nee-ad'-zom-ahee)[84] verb

1. to dream:
    i) have visions in dreams (Acts 2:17; the second dream in *"dreams will dream"*)
    ii) of false prophets (Jude 8)

Hebrew: Vision/Visions

מַרְאָה *marah* (mar-aw')[85] noun

1. a vision as means of revelation (Nm 12:6; 1 Sm 3:15; Gn 46:2; Ez 43:3; Dn 10:16).

מַרְאֶה *mareh* (mar-eh')[86] noun

1. **sight, appearance, vision:**

  i) sight, phenomenon, spectacle (Ex 3:3)
  ii) appearance (Gn 2:9)
  iii) appearance, sight, vision (Nm 8:4)

2) **what is seen** (Is 11:3)
3) **a supernatural vision** (Ez 8:4; 43:3)
4) **sight, vision** (Eccl 6:9)

Both *marah* and *mareh* are derived from the common verb *ra'ah*, meaning "to see."

מַחֲזֶה *machazeh* (makh-az-eh')[87] noun

1. **vision:**

  i) vision, in an ecstatic state (Ez 13:7; Nm 24:4,16; Gn 15:1)

חָזוֹן *chazon* (khaw-zone')[88] noun

1. **a vision:**

  i) as seen in the ecstatic state (Mi 3:6; Ez 12:24)
  ii) vision in the night (Is 29:7)
  iii) divine communication in a vision, oracle, prophesy (Ez 7:26; 2 Chr 32:32; Is 29:7; Ez 12:27; Dn 8:1)
  iv) vision, as title of book of prophecy (Na 1:1; Is 1:1)

חִזָּיוֹן *chizzayon* (khiz-zaw-yone')[89] noun

1. **vision:**

  i) vision, in the ecstatic state (2 Sm 7:17; Is 22:1,5)
  ii) vision in the night (Jb 4:13; 20:8; 33:15)
  iii) divine communication in a vision, oracle, prophecy (2 Sm 7:17; Jb 33:15; Jl 2:28)

חָזוּת *chazuth* (khaw-zooth')[90] noun

1. **vision, conspicuousness:**
    i) vision, oracle of a prophet (Is 21:2)
    ii) conspicuousness in appearance (Dn 8:5,8)

חֵזֶו *chezev* (Aramaic: khay'-zev)[91] noun

1. **vision, appearance:**
    i) vision (as mode of revelation) (Dn 2:19; 7:1,2)
    ii) appearance (Dn 7:20)

Greek: Vision/Visions

ὅραμα *horama* (hor'-am-ah)[92] noun

1. **supernatural visions, whether asleep or awake:**
    i) vision (Mt 17:9; Acts 7:31)
2. **the state of being while receiving a vision** (in the day as in Acts 10:3; 9:10,12 or in the night as in Acts 16:9; 18:9)

ὅρασις *horasis* (hor'-as-is)[93] noun

1. **that which is seen:**
    i) appearance
    ii) of supernatural vision (Acts 2:17)

ὀπτασία *optasia* (op-tas-ee'-ah)[94] noun

1. **a vision,** of that which the deity permits a human being to see, either of his own divine being, or of something else usually hidden from men (Lk 1:22; 24:23; 2 Cor 12:1)

Conclusion

What does all this mean? Look at some of the interesting observations from the above information.

The Hebrew verb *chalam* means activity of dreaming ordinary dreams during sleep, but it is also used for dreams with prophetic meaning or dreams of false prophets. The Hebrew noun *chalom* refers to a dream during sleep which may have prophetic meaning and again can be a dream used by false prophets. The verb *chalam* and the noun *chalom* have almost the same meanings. This is an example of the various factors that effect word usage, as mentioned in the introduction to this Key Words Study, such as author style, audience, and cultural setting.

The Greek noun *onar* means a dream and is found only in Matthew. The Greek noun *enupnion* means a dream. The Greek verb *enupniazomai* means to dream whereby one has visions in dreams and can also be used by false prophets.

The Hebrew noun *marah* is a vision, a means of revelation. The noun *mareh* is a sight, appearance, vision, and it pertains to what is seen and can be a supernatural vision according to its use in Scripture. The noun *machazeh* is a vision in an ecstatic state. The Hebrew noun *chazon* means a vision which is seen in the ecstatic state. It can also be a vision in the night and can be a means of divine communication, as in an oracle or prophesy. *Chazon* can also be a vision, as the title of the book of prophecy. It is interesting to note that the Hebrew noun *chizzayon* has almost the same meanings as *chazon*— a vision in the ecstatic state. It can be a vision received at night. Divine communication, as in an oracle or prophecy, is sometimes involved in the vision. This is another example of the various factors that affect word usage such as authorship, audience, and culture.

The Greek noun *horama* is a supernatural vision, whether asleep or awake. The Greek noun *optasia* is a vision of that which the deity permits a human being to see, either of his own divine being or something else usually hidden from men.

There is another interesting Hebrew verb—*chalam*—that is worth special mention. Generally, it has the meaning "to dream."

But as the verb stems change in the language, *chalam* in the *Qal* stem means, "their young are healthy,"[94] and in the *Hiphil* stem, "and restore me to health."[95] This presents a challenge to our thinking and so the question is asked: Can healing come through dreams and visions? This seems to confirm the findings of science— that we must dream to be mentally and emotionally healthy.

Dreams and visions are two distinct experiences with similarities. The distinction is that dreams come to us as we sleep, while visions come as a more direct intrusion into a moment of time while we are awake, such as during a trance.[96] The similarity between dreams and visions is found in the language of the message. Both dreams and visions present us with a message comprised of a sequence of images, symbols, sounds, and emotions with meaning, clarity, and purpose.

For the purposes of this book, we believe the approach we teach to understanding dreams can also be applied to the interpretation of visions.

In summary, scriptural words must be seen in their context. Just as the word "bridge" has many different meanings, the only one that counts is the one relevant to the context in which it is being used. Biblical authorship and intended audience and cultural setting influence the use, meaning, and understanding of words used in the Bible. Much can be understood by studying the original languages of the Bible.

Endnotes

1 Jl 2:28.

2 Sandford, John L. *The Elijah Task*. Tulsa, OK, Victory House Inc., 1977, p. 169.

3 Dt 26:17.

4 Jn 10:27.

5 1 Cor 14:1.

6 In the conclusion of his talk to a 1960 meeting of the American Psychiatric Association, Dr. Dement said,

> "We believe that if anyone were deprived of dreams long enough, it might result in some sort of catastophic breakdown."

—Sanford, John A., *Dreams: God's Forgotten Language*, New York, New York, HarperCollins, 1989, p. 121.

7 "Dream." *Britannica 2001 Deluxe Edition. CD-ROM* © 1994–2001, Britannica.com Inc.

8 "Trance." *The New Oxford Dictionary of English*. © Oxford University Press, 1999.

9 Acts 10:9–17; 22:17–21.

10 Acts 10:17,19.

[11] "Consciousness, States of." *Microsoft® Encarta® Encyclopedia 2000.* © 1993-1999 Microsoft Corporation. All rights reserved.

[12] CNN archives; October 8, 2001; Posted: 3:36 p.m. EDT (19:36 GMT).

[13] Acts 2:17.

[14] 2 Kgs 6:8 ff.

[15] "Dreaming." *Microsoft® Encarta® 96 Encyclopedia.* © 1993-1995, Microsoft Corporation. All rights reserved. © Funk & Wagnalls Corporation. All rights reserved.

[16] Riffel, Herman. *Dream Interpretation.* Shippensburg, PA: Destiny Image Publishers, 1993, p. 12.

[17] Sandford, John and Mark. *Deliverance and Inner Healing.* Grand Rapids: Chosen Books, 1992, p. 206.

[18] Gn 37:11.

[19] Gn 42:9.

[20] Gn 40:8.

[21] Gn 41:47ff.

[22] Acts 10:44.

[23] Acts 2:4.

[24] Ex 34:7, Nm 14:18, Jer 32:18.

[25] Lv 26:40.

[26] Mt 12:29,43–45.

[27] Mt 26:41.

[28] *Defrag* or *defragment* means "to bring order to the information on a hard drive."

[29] "Incubus." *The New Oxford Dictionary of English.* © Oxford University Press, 1999.

[30] "Succubus." *The New Oxford Dictionary of English.* © Oxford University Press, 1999.

[31] "Incubus." *Britannica 2001 Deluxe Edition. CD-ROM* Copyright © 1994-2001, Britannica.com Inc.

32 Riffel, Herman. *Dreams: Wisdom Within*, p. 117.

33 Eph 4:11–12.

34 John Paul Jackson, in his tape series *Understanding Dreams & Visions*, looks at who is the focus in the dream to determine where the dream is **intrinsic** (subjective).

35 Gn 40:5–8.

36 John Paul Jackson, in his tape series *Understanding Dreams & Visions*, looks at who is the focus in the dream to determine where the dream is **extrinsic** (objective).

37 Dn 7.

38 Gn 41.

39 Dn 7:28.

40 Dn 8:26.

41 Rv 1:11.

42 Gn 18:17 ff.

43 Lk 19:17.

44 Gn 37:7.

45 Is 9:6.

46 Gal 1:17.

47 Gal 1:21.

48 Acts 11:26.

49 Acts 13:1–3.

50 Gn 31:10–13.

51 Riffel, Herman. *Dream Interpretation*. p. 2.

52 "Dreams as Extensions of the Waking State." *Britannica 2001 Deluxe Edition. CD-ROM*, copyright © 1994-2001, Britannica.com Inc.

53 Olson, Dave and Linda. *Listening Prayer*. Corona, CA: Self Published, 1997.

54 Sandford, John L. *Training for the Ministry of Prayer Counseling*. Post Falls, ID: Elijah House, 1997.

[55] Smith, Dr. Ed., *Beyond Tolerable Recovery*. Campbellsville, KY: Family Care Publishing, 1997.

[56] McNutt, Dr. Francis, *School of Healing Prayer*. Jacksonville, FL: Christian Healing Ministries, 1999.

[57] Lk 10:27.

[58] Bauer, Walter. *A Greek-English Lexicon of the New Testament—and Other Early Christian Literature*. Second Edition. Chicago: The University of Chicago Press, 1979. Page 555.

[59] Mt 4:19.

[60] Rom 3:23.

[61] Is 59:2.

[62] Rom 6:23.

[63] 2 Cor 5:21.

[64] 1 Jn 1:9.

[65] Lk 11:13.

[66] Jn 14:26.

[67] Rom 10:10.

[68] "Reading (activity)." *Microsoft® Encarta® Encyclopedia 2000*. © 1993-1999 Microsoft Corporation. All rights reserved.

[69] "Metaphor." *The American Heritage® Dictionary of the English Language, Third Edition*. Copyright © 1992 by Houghton Mifflin Company. Electronic version licensed from InfoSoft International, Inc. All rights reserved.

[70] Ibid., "Simile."

[71] Ibid., "Metonymy."

[72] "Parable." *The American Heritage® Dictionary of the English Language, Third Edition*. Copyright © 1992 by Houghton Mifflin Company. Electronic version licensed from InfoSoft International, Inc. All rights reserved.

[73] Jn 21:22.

[74] Mt 28:20, Heb 13:5–6.

[75] Eph 4:11–13.

76 Gn 3:12–13.

77 Is 9:6.

78 Eph 4:27.

79 Brown, Francis, S. R. Driver, Charles A. Briggs. *A Hebrew and English Lexicon of the Old Testament*. Oxford, England: Clarendon Press, Oxford University Press, 1978. p. 321 b.

80 Ibid., p. 321 c.

81 Ibid., p. 1093 a.

82 Bauer, *A Greek-English Lexicon,* Second Edition, p. 569.

83 Ibid., p. 270 c.

84 Ibid.

85 Brown, Driver, Briggs. *A Hebrew and English Lexicon of the Old Testament.* p. 909 b.

86 Ibid., p. 909 d.

87 Ibid., p. 303 d.

88 Ibid., p. 303 a.

89 Ibid., p. 303 b.

90 Ibid., p. 303 b.

91 Ibid., p. 1092 d.

92 Bauer, *A Greek-English Lexicon,* Second Edition. p. 577 b.

93 Ibid., p. 577 c.

94 Ibid., p. 576 c.

95 Jb 39:4.

96 Is 38:16.

97 Acts 11:5.

Bibliography

KEY WORDS BIBLIOGRAPHY

Aland, Barbara, Kurt Aland, Hohannes Karavidopoulos, Carlo Martini, Bruce Metzger. *The Greek New Testament*. Stuttgart, Germany: Biblia-Druck, 1994.

Bauer, Walter. *A Greek-English Lexicon of the New Testament—and Other Early Christian Literature*. Second Edition. Chicago, IL: The University of Chicago Press, 1979.

Brown, Colin. *The New International Dictionary of New Testament Theology*. Grand Rapids, MI: Zondervan Publishing House, 1979.

Brown, Francis, S. R. Driver, Charles A. Briggs. *A Hebrew and English Lexicon of the Old Testament*. Oxford, England: Clarendon Press, Oxford University Press, 1978.

Elliger, K. W. Rudoph, ed. *Biblia Hebraica Stuttgartensia*. Stuttgart, Germany: German Bible Society, 1990.

Harris, R., L. Gleason, L. Archer, Bruce K. Waltke, *The Theological Wordbook of the Old Testament*. Chicago, IL: Moody Press, 1980.

Strongs, James. *Strong's Complete Dictionary of Bible Words*. Nashville, TN: Thomas Nelson Publishers, 1966.

Thayer, Joseph. *A Greek-English Lexicon of the New Testament*. Nashville, TN: Broadman Press, 1977.

Vine, W. E. *Vine's Expository Dictionary of Old and New Testament Words*. New Jersey: Fleming H. Revell Company, 1981.

DREAMS BIBLIOGRAPHY

Books

Conner, Kevin J. *Interpreting the Symbols and Types*. Portland, OR: City Bible Publishing, 1992.

Deere, Jack. *Surprised by the Voice of God*. Grand Rapids, MI: Zondervan Publishing, 1996.

Hamon, Jane. *Dreams and Visions*. California, USA: Regal Books, 2000.

Milligan, Ira L. *Every Dreamer's Handbook*. Shippensburg, PA: Treasure House, Destiny Image Publishers, 2000.

Owen, W. Stuart. *A Dictionary of Bible Symbols*. London England: Grace Publications, 1992.

Riffel, Herman. *Dream Interpretation*. Shippensburg, PA: Destiny Image Publishers, 1993.

Riffel, Herman. *Dreams: Wisdom Within*. Shippensburg, PA: Destiny Image Publishers, 1990.

Ryle, James. *A Dream Come True*. Lake Mary, FL: Creation House, 1996.

Sandford, John L. and Paula Sandford. *The Elijah Task*. Tulsa, OK: Victory House, Inc., 1977.

Sanford, John A. *Dreams: God's Forgotten Language*. New York, NY: HarperCollins Publishers, 1989.

Sanford, John and Mark. *Deliverance and Inner Healing*. Grand Rapids, MI: Chosen Books, 1992. HarperCollins Publishers, 1989.

Thomas, Benny. *Exploring the World of Dreams*. New Kensington, PA: Whitaker House, 1990.

Audio Tapes

Jackson, John Paul. *Understanding Dreams & Visions*. Fort Worth, TX: Streams Ministries International, date unknown.

Riffel, Herman. *Christian Dream Interpretation*. Elma, NY: Communion with God Ministries Publishers, 1992.

ENCYCLOPEDIA ENTRIES

Hema, John and Jacob Arlow. "Psychoanalysis." *Microsoft Encarta 96 Encyclopedia*. Funk & Wagnalls Corporation, Microsoft Corporation, 1996.

Hartmann, Ernest. "Dreaming." *Microsoft Encarta 96 Encyclopedia*. Funk & Wagnalls Corporation, Microsoft Corporation, 1996.

About the Authors

For a number of years now, Steve and Dianne have been growing in their understanding of God's heart for dreams. They believe the subject of dreams has been taken by the secular world for its own purposes. Together, they want to be part of God's move to reclaim this vital means of communication for his Kingdom and his people.

Being dreamers and pastoral counselors themselves, Steve and Dianne bring personal experience to this area and want to offer the keys they have gathered so others can walk in the fullness of what God has for them.

Steve and Dianne have taught internationally on the subject of dreams, inner healing, and renewal.

Dianne Bydeley, B.A., B.Ed., M.Ed., MCS, C.P.C.

Steve Bydeley, C.E.T., C.P.C.

Lapstone Ministries

...is a cross-denominational ministry working to draw the Body of Christ into a deeper relationship with God and each other. Steve and Dianne are the founders and directors of Lapstone Ministries.

Resources Available by Steve and Dianne

- *Dream Dreams* book
- *Dream Dreams* workbook (a companion to *Dream Dreams* for individual application and group study)
- Audio cassette — 5-tape set
- VHS cassette — 4-tape set
- Internet dream interpretation mentoring — 12 weeks

Booking Seminars

We are available for a variety of formats of Dream Seminars. For information on our seminars, ordering books, workbooks, or cassettes, etc., contact:

Website: www.lapstoneministries.org

E-mail: info@lapstoneministries.org